2nd ID

Jun Namgoong

WHERE SEOUL & SHANGHAI MEET

Cover art by the author

ISBN 979-11-969529-8-3

Published by DIGLASIA

For my sister

Contents

PART 2 - Reorientation

"A baby is not afraid of the uncertainty, because they have not conceptualised the meaning of consequences of action. So they are not afraid of making mistakes, hence, consequences. They live in the absence of understanding the meaning of failure or mistakes and their impacts. They learn it later, the instant they make their first failure and mistake in their life. The switch of fear gets turned on, and the sensitivity of the sensor will be increasing to the extent that any slightest possibility of physical and mental touch will turn it on."

"When people say you are too old to learn something, it actually means that you have lost neural plasticity or, in a rather simple term, the ability to pick up a skill easily. But… why? How did we lose one of the most important and distinct human capabilities? And how can we regain that?"

"Remember your origin but do not dwell on it"

Preface

I have put down my pencil and closed my laptop many times to reach this point of being able to write about something that's still uncertain for me. Tossing in my bed in the midst of many early mornings, a question kept coming to me: 'Am I qualified to write on this subject?'

It took me about several years to grab that pencil again. During those years, I had contemplated the possibility of being able to explain my experiences as an adult learner of a second language. I was 24 when I was starting out, and 38 now. I'd dedicated about 15 years of my adulthood to mastering my second language. Though, maybe the word 'master' is a bit strong, as we never really master anything in our lives. The thought has occasionally lingered in my head, however, which keeps my obsession with language intact.

When I made the decision to study Applied Linguistics with two things in my mind. Primarily, it was my wish to find someone or precedents that would teach me academic terminologies to elaborate my experience. I wished to learn from someone whom I expected would be more experienced multilingual. Although I detested the conventions of education system, I desperately wished to meet with such a person who would shed light on the mysteries of acquiring a language and who would be capable of elaborating my second language acquisition process. I certainly did not wish to interact with someone who would be such pedantic scholars who would stick their nose on the text books. I regret to say that all I've learnt from school elementary to master's is how to properly use relevant terminologies and references that are written by dare-devils who actually experienced what they wrote. I regret to inform you potential university students thinking about doing a social science program that writing research papers only taught me about the usage of the academic writing formats and how to properly organise the contents of the paper so that I wouldn't wear out the readers (professors) eyes. The problem was that because the rules of academic writing were so rigorous that I felt that my intuition was slowly fading away. Consequently, my major concern went from writing an experiential paper to meeting the criteria. I wondered why is it that a professor who can only speak one language can teach hundreds of grown-ups when a child with much better intuitional capability to learn languages cannot? Because children do not know all terminologies?

Something has gone wrong. Seriously wrong.

The underlying principles of human psychology, mainly, consciousness. The so-called gut feelings or instincts, once labelled in scientific terms, it's interpreted within a limited scope or circle. What our heart tells us to do in find solutions to problems is usually right for most of the time. And What we will find and how we will find it are really a matter of individual.

As I realised this, I experienced intermittent dilemmas. I found myself reading through dull and dim literature where most of the discussion centre around survey questions and answers that I believed could easily be manipulated. I ended up learning hundreds of terminologies and jargons which led me to the conclusion that verbalisation cannot embody experience. It was that moment I realised the reason for the existence of many forms of art—all of which have a common purpose—to express one's experience in a best possible way because whether it be of physical or abstract, but the complete embodiment of an experience cannot be achieved. The current means of communication is certainly not enough. We don't have the science as seen in the movie, "Matrix" where a perfect virtual world fires up all of our neutrons and senses as if it's real. So let us be aware of the limitations in sharing one's experience by verbalisation because it certainly limits the scope of knowledge to how the words are interpreted by you and accepted conventionally in a given society.

My feelings of insecurity, of being in doubt about if I were qualified to write on the subject vanished when I noticed professors who claimed that they knew so much about what it takes to acquire a language, while only speaking one language themselves. I have never seen some of the most renown professors of linguistics (such as Noam Chomsky) speak another language besides their mother tongue. They have written many books, publishing literature about language acquisition, but I haven't had the honour of seeing those great professors actually speak another language besides their first. I am sure some of them may be able to, and they are not just all talk, but most scholars in academic circles are too engrossed in publishing papers on their 'discoveries' or 'findings from their research.' To use a bit of an analogy, if acquiring another language is a sport, those famed scholars would be like expert commentators and spectators, doing nothing but watching, paying attention to every move of the athletes on the field. I have been one of those athletes. I've been on the field actually drilling and hammering it out; this fact alone led me to the conclusion that I am absolutely qualified to write about it.

There was, however, another thing that concerned me: the fact that my journey had taken 15 years. I feared the possibility that the amount of work involved in the process of acquiring another language would sound too dreadful, potentially scaring people away, especially those who believe in the mainstream, popular language courses promising shortcuts.

In any event, acquiring another language in adulthood can be a rewarding experience – that is, if you have achieved some level of fluency. It is more likely that the countless hours of reciting words and phrases will not pay off. Every year, we see the publication of scores of language books, with hundreds of copies churned out as if it's fashion. This selection just makes us all the more confused: we ask, 'Which book? Which course? Which app?' Stacks of books pile up on our shelves, but, when we truly think about it, we realize we only know bits and fragments of the language – it's not an integral part of us. Every time we catch sight of these books, the sense of disappointment and regret rushes back.

Observation, imitation and Intuitionally coming into one's own are the most powerful built-in learning tools that current science cannot explain. Academic literature particularly those summarising the results of surveys cannot account for all individuals' experiences. The primary reason for such is that some people neither want to share nor feel the need to get noticed. They are those creative people who are already content with their lives, living to the fullest while being private. They are too busy to bother getting involved in academic circles. They learn like wild animals and devour knowledge by experience; a nature that certainly does not fit well around academia. The idea of being on a linguistics text book as a research subject is of utter oddity for them. As a result, we rarely hear about them. It is because they have come to understand things in their own way. They have come to develop their own learning methods that work best for themselves. They know that generalising and narrowing down individuals' experience by survey or research, in which the participants only give half-hearted answers, are certainly not reliable source of wisdom. They know that there are many anonymously amazing people out there who already know the truth, but do not know academic terminologies to 'elaborate' their experiences do not bother looking at flamboyant fatty papers. They might appear to be ignorant but the truth is they know how to employ intuition in a way that science cannot explain.

What has happened here? Think for a second. What's happened is that, over time, we have developed excessive dependency on external resources – rather than our inner minds and intuition – when it comes to learning. Why? What causes that behaviour? What's killed the child-like brain that we all used to have? How can we possibly get it back so that we can learn like children again, while taking full advantage of our adult brains?

As you might have noticed by now, this book is not a language course book. It is a book designed for you to awaken the inner linguistic intuition that has long been dormant deep inside of you. I acknowledge that finding your own best ways to learn things may be the best approach, however, as most of our genes are known to be mostly the same (99%), we are genetically designed to learn certain things in certain ways, namely the senses. In this book, the five senses are descried as the primary learning tools and rest is secondary. Terminologies used in Applied Linguistics or Neuroscience are minimised for obvious reasons. I emphasise experiential knowledge and following one's intuitional belief are the most powerful and effective in learning a second language as our senses are the master of our mind. So do not read it religiously; I cannot possibly touch your senses.

PART 1

Mentality for Acquisition

My Rules, Not Yours

1. Be open to possibilities.
2. Imagine, fantasise, and romanticise on a daily basis throughout your journey. Keep them up-to-date as you work your way up.
3. To learn a language means that we will use our innate cognitive and physical capacities, just like learning a new skill. To acquire a language, however, means that we have become inseparable from it.
4. Mind and body are connected.
5. Manageable, exciting, and slightly challenging goals prompt us to take action.
6. Subgoals provide daily motivation towards bigger goals.
7. When the goal seems unmanageable or out of our control, we tend to give up.
8. Breaking a rigid routine can bring in fresh air.
9. Initially, reservations have no place in language learning.

10. One of the most difficult challenges for adult language learners to overcome and master is knowing the right time and place to employ their logical or analytic minds.
11. For some, a sense of uncertainty engenders curiosity and excitement to learn.
12. Predictability kills motivation.
13. Surprises are more unforgettable.
14. It all starts with courage and a break from the dogmatic belief deep inside you.
15. Identify with the language and culture, but don't sweat on it.

Chapter 1

Know Your Place

"The ability to learn anything so easily and spontaneously has been degenerated under the rigid social system that imposes restraints on our natural creativity to learn, ultimately conditioning us to be a tamed communal animal."

Since your birth, everything you've seen out there, every human interaction you've engaged in with the people you've met has been carried out in your first language. You've become acquainted with and/or befriended thousands of people. There have been many unforgettable, tearful moments – your birth, your first fight in kindergarten with your best friend with whom you're still in touch, school field trips to cities that you had been itching to visit, and your first love back in high school, who could now possibly be your wife, reading this book with you in the comfort of your living room. You remember your first part-time job at McDonalds, KFC, or Burger King. Some of you might have gone through heartbreaking moments with deaths of loved ones. Maybe you're nearing the end on your life, reading this book only for entertainment. I don't know who you are, but I'd like to share something that I have treasured.

I once tried hard to fit in, acting like a cool, westernised Asian guy from somewhere in the Far East. I didn't even know the meaning of the phrase 'national anthem' when my friend asked about my own. It was embarrassing when I realised the meaning in my first language. I once thought that the only way to learn a foreign language was to neglect my own, getting immersed in the other culture – which was partly right, because I learnt a ton in a relatively short time. I made friends with people from all over the world, working hard to learn the language and reviewing everything at my desk every night.

At one point, I realised I had not been in contact with my own countrymen for almost a few years, meaning I had not spoken my first language (except at times when I made the occasional phone call to my family). In school, I resisted the temptation to mingle with people who would possibly trigger a switch to my first language. When I passed by the school canteen, I would often see a group of people sitting around a big round table, engaged in a conversation in my first language—they looked comfortable, like they felt at home in that tiny social circle. Deep down, there certainly was a tingling sensation in me gravitating towards them, but I managed to keep the urge under control. I have to admit there were moments when my reasoning gave in to the sensation of comfort and familiarity. I would stop walking, hesitating for a few full seconds, my instincts telling me to join the group. For most of the time, though, my ability to reason would put a stop to that momentary urge, and my *perseverance* would soon regain control. In reminiscing, I vividly remember those people for how happy, relaxed, and natural they looked in those confines—the look of how they would express themselves without wracking their brains. I remember that, most of the time, I would turn and march away with my teeth clenched. I knew that, in order for my second language to supplant my first, I'd have to live it for as many years as I lived in another world.

Integral Part of Your life

I consider language learning to be life; life that is being simultaneously translated into the sounds and texts on which we survive and rely. Without life and the motivation to communicate the matters of life, language would never have existed. We all know that languages are different in one way or another, and that there are lots of variables that make them unique, such as geographical, climate, and political differences accounting for varying degrees of living conditions and social structures, creating a wide range of culturally unique items, whether physical or abstract. Therefore, some traditions cannot even be translated into another language. Other languages don't have names for our traditions. We have to borrow words, or we loan our own to others. This is because we produce language *primarily to express the existence or presence of things or ideas in our immediate surroundings.*

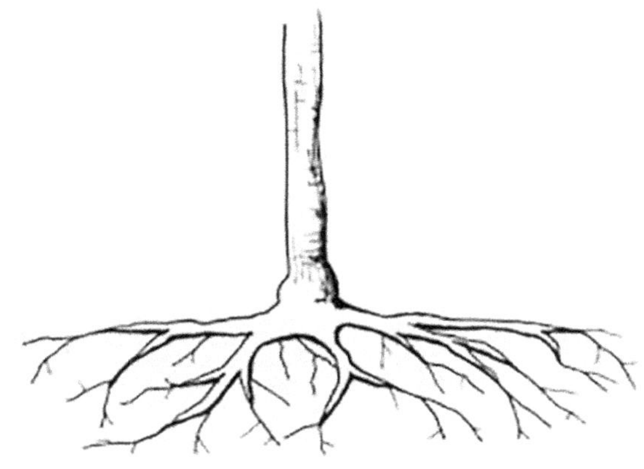

What is a language then? Languages represent our lifestyles, and *we use them to communicate existing things and thoughts around us.* They tell us so much about our roots. They tell us where we are originally from, our ancestry, or lineage, which we often neglect when we are learning a foreign language.

Inherited Traits

Our roots have a wide network of underground branches, spreading deep and wide in all directions. It is *an intricate system from which our genes stem and give nourishment to our physical, mental, and behavioural development.* These roots of genetic codes *embody our ancestry; hence, they are fixed in place.* The codes won't change easily, as they have been passed down for thousands of years. At birth, the codes predispose our physical and mental behaviour. We have inherited these genetic codes, written long before we were born, and this, in essence, preconditions our prospective personality traits after birth.

If your mother is a professor and well-versed in literature, or if your father is a neurosurgeon who understands and performs the complexities of his vocation's practices, there is a good chance that you will be good at the kinds of jobs requiring traits similar to the ones in their occupations.

In the context of language learning, if your ancestry has no record of ever living in a multilingual environment, it's likely that you lack the particular genetic element necessary to live in that particular kind of environment. In contrast, suppose your ancestors had already made the enormous effort, struggling to become bilingual before you were born. They'd done it to survive in places where people spoke more than one language. What would happen if people like this passed their genes down to you?

Your genes are already *preconditioned* to learn more than one language, making it easier for you to acquire languages than for those who don't have such ancestral roots. But, that's only when you *try to utilise the inherited traits. If you don't use them, you will lose them.*

Why the distinction between inherited or not? Because it gives us a clue as to what we are, where we are, and what has to be done in order for us to acquire another language. If your ancestors had only lived in a monolingual environment, you may not have the innate ability to speak multiple languages. It means that, if you like to be multilingual, you will be the sole person responsible *for evolving beyond what has been given to you.* You will be *responsible for developing new habits, continuously modifying your behaviour in order to cross beyond the parameters of your birth.*

Is it possible to rewrite our existing genetic codes?

Some linguists claim that human beings are predisposed to have the innate ability to pick up their mother tongues. In some sense, this genetic predisposition theory may hold some drops of water, as we can imagine that thousands of years of permanent residency in one particular region have well-shaped our muscles – the diaphragm, vocal cords, and nearly all that internal organs that are required to produce sounds and conceptualise our immediate surroundings. The brain we inherited has been optimised for this particular environment. Our physical features, particularly those used for oral functions, have been pre-designed or shaped by our genes as a result of years of adaptation. So, there is some truth to the theory that, when we were born, our brains were already wired in certain ways. The claim that our brain has been fossilised, however, is non-sensical, as each generation has had to adapt to the ever-changing environment, generating a new set of genes.

What should be of interest for discussion in public discourse now is that, every time an *adaptation* occurs, the change *overwrites the existing genetic codes.* It's my belief – and I am certain there are others who are on the same page – that we can evolve beyond what's given to us by pushing our boundaries to become multilingual. But then, how?

Chapter 2

Who Are You?

When I think about how I've gotten this far as a language learner, I feel like a tree, with its growth stages, is the best way to describe the acquisition process, as it can be used to illustrate the chronological stages of language learning.

Roots

The roots of a tree show its place of origin, where it was born – you may call it lineage. The roots are where we inherit genetic codes from our ancestors which have been preconditioned and modified by past time periods. Our ancestors had to adapt to the ever-changing environment, developing traits and skills necessary both for survival and advancement. As part of this process, the genetic codes have been renewed and rewritten from generation to generation, as each lifetime has a unique living environment with its own requirements for survival. Therefore, at birth, our genetics were already a complex-yet-pragmatic network of behavioural elements essentially made to help us continue existing in the place of our origin. And it is this inherited predisposition that initially dictates our behaviour and patterns of thinking. From this, we can formulate a reasonably investigable query: Is it possible for us to go beyond what's given? Is it possible to rewrite our inherited bio-bahavioural traits if we intentionally change our living environment, or move to a place that is radially different from the scene of our origin?

YES, but only if you understand the following explanation and how to apply these principles to your own unique existence.

Where Are You Now?

Now, locate yourself on a world map, and begin examining your roots. What are they? What ideologies have seeped into your head? Is your culture and language based on Confucianism or Christianity? Does your language reflect a historical relationship with neighbouring countries? Do you share certain cultural elements with those neighbors? Is your country as geographically isolated as North Korea? What is your identity, and how do people from outside your home perceive you or your nation? Know your place, and start from there.

Jun Namgoong

A Rebel's Advantage as a Language Learner

A language is the embodiment of a culture. If your perspectives are not fully tied up in your culture, you will likely have success as you start learning a second language. If you are a loyalist to your culture and its traditions, you will face much more difficulty in changing your behaviour to learn another language. This is because your behaviour has been optimised to function within the society of your first language. Following this logic, we can speculate that culturally or politically conservative adults may not be ideal language learners, because their minds run strictly and narrowly within the confines of one particular culture. In contrast, adults with mind-sets rebellious against many aspects of their cultures of origin may make good language learners, especially if they are learning a language whose culture allows them to express things that their first language cannot. For instance, you, as an American, may feel that people in your country should be more polite in social settings or public places, so you often find yourself wishing you could express yourself in a more respectful manner to honour another person. Unfortunately, your first language does not provide the ability to do that. You then turn to other languages – such as Japanese, Korean, or Javanese – where the use of honourifics is common and necessary to function in society.

Beginner's luck, however, only lasts until we face another block: cultural dogma. All languages are imposing forces that dictate our behaviour. We will come to the realisation that, no matter what languages we speak, the dogmas of culture will eventually get in the way of our creativity, dominating our minds.

Chapter 3

The Death of Innate Inventiveness

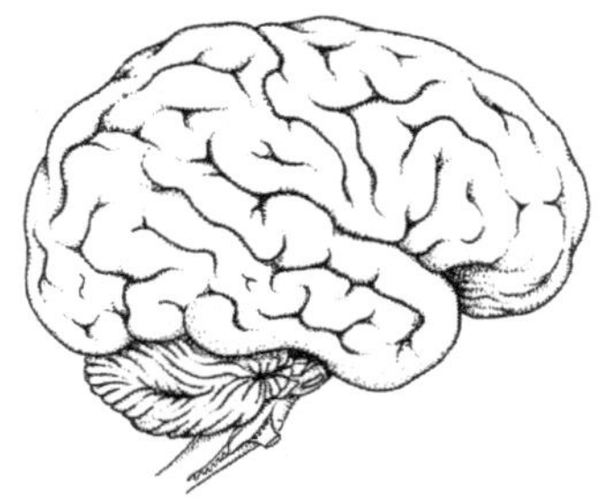

How Did We Lose Innate Inventiveness (Linguistic Creativity)?

As adults, we must ensure that we have acknowledged and understood the effects of the cultural dogmas on our minds and our cognitive developments. It is this aspect of our culture that freezes our neuro-plasticity. It's systematically orchestrated by enforcing collective, patterned behaviour and ways of thinking, while suppressing our natural desires to think outside the box, such as inventing new patterns and novel ways of making a living. Ask yourself the following question:

What led us to the point of losing our creativity? When did it begin, and why did we let it happen?

EXPERIMENT.
FAIL.
LEARN.
REPEAT.

We can find the answer simply by observing the stages of how small children acquire their first languages. Initially, they are allowed to be creative with language, playing with words and syntax. They do not realise their grammatical mistakes, so they come up with new rules, misplacing subjects, verbs, and objects, and assembling sentences in puzzling orders. The experimental period indicates that children will keep searching for ways to express themselves from very creative angles, because their minds are open to all forms of communication, even if they do not follow the conventions of the language. Their creativity with language will come to an end when *authorities* get involved in the learning process and start correcting the learners. After years of repeated exposure to the same environment, where fixed patterns of the environment's language were drilled into their heads, their patterns of thinking also become solidified – the same goes for their behaviour. Think for a second. Why do people with slight autism tend to be geniuses? It's because they do not rely on language to express themselves. Likewise, creative people do not solely rely on language. They use all possible means of communication, as they're aware that a language can limit us to fixed ways of thinking.

The principles of our immediate living environments dominate the development of our minds, and our natural inclination is to merely blend in. We see that everyone around us is on board;

there is no reason for us to jump off the ship, into the sea of the unknown, or to become alienated from the comfortable unity. This is how we establish the belief of what's normal and abnormal, and of what is to be accepted and what is not. All of that occurs within the confines of our original cultures. As such cultural norms and traditions are present at all times, we must adjust our behaviour accordingly. In other words, we become tamed by the collective system, and our first language exists to embody the system and maintain the patterns of collective thinking and behaviour in society. Consequently, when we hear a language that does not represent anything in our culture, we immediately recognise it as abnormal or simply tune it out.

Naturally then, acquiring another language means learning how to expressing another culture; the degree of cultural difference will dictate the degree of difficulty. Japanese and Chinese languages are easier for Koreans to learn because they share many common cultural and ideological components, whereas Italians learn French much more easily than Chinese people do.

Imposing Living Environment

A child won't perceive the process of learning a language as compulsory, because the living environment is the most common and intensive context in which language is naturally learnt. The child's immediate surroundings have already been shaped, weathered, reshaped, and renovated numerous times by their predecessors. Language is readily available, representing this dynamic, ever-changing environment. Most of the time, the child won't have to seek out learning materials to understand context, because his living environment is the context itself (immersive) and the people around the child will explain things or, at least, talk about them. If the child is curious, able to pay special attention to what's being said and the situation in which it is said, he will pick up on contextual clues and understand the meaning after repeated exposure. As children, we did not even realise we were learning language, as our environments dictated how we learned. We simply gravitated towards all the physical and linguistic manifestations of our culture, conceptualising and synthesising cultural elements with the linguistic components that represent them.

When we start learning our first language, every word we produce is relevant to our immediate surroundings, as we can only express our immediate needs or urgent desires – basic necessities for survival. We do not have the ability to think in abstract ways yet, relying largely on visuals. Our visually rich natural environment helps us seamlessly conceptualise the world as something we perceive as it shows. When we become able to recall the names of the objects we see, we can refer to them without them being in sight. Until then, the child's brain will concentrate all energy and attention on achieving one particular goal: learning the language to satisfy urgent desires that will be immediately rewarding. With such concentration, the child will learn the language relatively easily.

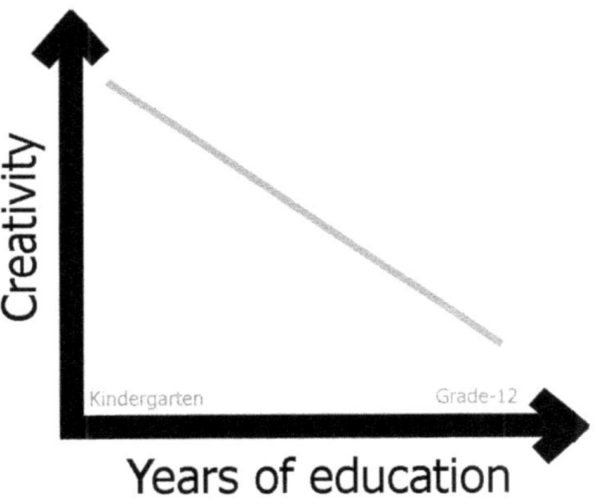

Every time he utters a word, he gets an immediate response (reward) from the masters of the language, parents or teachers. It is easier, because the child's brain is in the state of suction, wide open, tirelessly observing all the happenings of everyday life, and sucking up minute visual details of physical information. That's because the child has a ceaseless burning desire and curiosity to make sense of the world, which means being able to communicate with members of a community. In the suction state, the mind is free from the contrasting thoughts or ideas that exist in the adult brain – simply because the child does not have past experiences for comparison. Precedents of experience are non-existent. Not knowing the meaning and consequences of failure (risk-taking), the child will have the best positive attitude (just give it a try) towards the most basic kind of language – the kind used to do tasks like eating, sleeping, making purchases, taking the bus, or using the toilet. Everyone around the child seems to adore him (acceptance). They are generous and forgiving (communal cooperation) when they interact with the child. Most importantly, they are willing to talk to the child (favour), sometimes correcting the child's language (proper instruction and reference) without judging (unbiased). And they do this free of charge (finance). The child will be introduced to new friends, playing with them in different public settings (variety), such as being on stage at a preschool talent show, talking with adults other than their parents for the first time, getting reprimanded by a teacher, or learning to measure the level of formality in language (common courtesy). As the child is exposed to a wide range of individuals and contexts, his knowledge of language grows naturally and exponentially.

As such, the environment of our origin provides all the cultural components that become directly connected to the language as we are exposed to them. All we have to do is to register them and then experiment with the language until we acquire it; of course, we do this subconsciously, unaware that we are even learning language. It's like somebody already furnished a new house before we moved in, and now we just live in there as if everything has been preconditioned for us. Our first language and cultural norms have been precomposed by our predecessors, and we, as successors, merely pick up where they left off, doing so without question. We simply accept it as is and pass it on to the next generation. The most fundamentally ideological features of language are learned without questioning. We just accept it as is.

Habit to Not Question

It is futile to question the reliability and preciseness of a language when the majority of those around us speak it. We rarely doubt the fallibility and efficiency of our first language. To invent new elements of a language, one will need the consensus of a majority of the members.

When we blindly accept and use what's readily available to us, our innate inventiveness with language and openness to novel approaches to communication die with it. It is from this point that the plasticity of the brain begins to tighten up to the point of dormancy due to the repression of the culture and the pressure of its norms. Our creativity regresses, eventually closing the door of possibility. Why question things? Why change? We can simply enjoy the entirety of the established whole for free; we do not have to strive to change the fundamental structure or lexical elements that perfectly represent our culture.

In most cases, change occurs only when our living environment or the masses demand it. In our first language acquisition, there is no individual originality. We are all imitative, submissive to the rigid structure of the language. To invent language, we would need to change, in some way, an aspect of the entire society. Think for a second. Who came up with the name "iPhone"? Did the invention change the entire structure of the language? The name was just added to the whole language. Sure, the new name rippled the surface of the water a bit, but the depths didn't even budge. This is the case when a linguistic development occurs in conjunction with a cultural development; the vocabulary and structure of a language will never change overnight. For this reason, when we are learning our first language, we must let our innate creativity grow weaker so that it will dissolve into the authority of the existing system. When that happens, we must listen to the masters of the language and imitate them in order to produce the same quality of language.

Nonetheless, children can't help being creative when they learn their first language, subconsciously trying variations of grammar and vocabulary by playing with the language. Their brains are such free-flowing entities, always talking to them, saying "Anything is possible" or "There are no rules." Without the awareness of social stigmas, restraints, a dogmatic belief system, or precedents in place, we can all be like children, because it is impossible to not be creative when there are no rules suppressing our natural creativity. Children, therefore, often attempt to create new words communicable to their intimate peers but often unintelligible to adults.

They do so to describe things for which they don't have words, paraphrasing self-righteously *until they are corrected, becoming more aware that there are consensual linguistic codes with which they must comply in order to be understood and accepted.* Until then, they play with words and invent phrases, while constantly being corrected and rephrased by the masters of the language in their environment. Each time they get corrected on the existing rules of the language by an imposing force, their strong urges to create and invent die down, bit-by-bit and day-by-day; this continues for years. Only once they realise the language items they have created are not conventionally acceptable or intelligible for the majority will they self-correct themselves to be validated, during which the fossilisation of the brain begins and neuroplasticity gradually fades away.

You, as an adult, have already gone through this stage of life. Let this reality sink into your head for a while. Reflect on it. What should you have to do now if you want to learn anything new?

Chapter 4

Developing Fear of Failures

School begins. Learning language is only easy until we start school. From there, we go on to learn more abstract ideas; that is, we begin to learn language that represents ideas beyond the scope of everyday physical matters. This is difficult, particularly for those who lack the foundational knowledge of and ability to recall pieces of language that represent everyday physical and visual objects. For most of us, though, our linguistic foundations allow us to use the correct phrases and sentences to communicate and understand thoughts in class. With this system in place, we start to gain knowledge, most of which is done without the benefit of experience. Through the use of textbook references, our knowledge of physical matters and abstract ideas grows exponentially across a range of subjects, while teachers and peers provide constant feedback on our performances, with the criticism forcing us to behave in certain ways. Our fluency of language nearly peaks, but at the expense of creativity or neuro-plasticity. At this point, we must note the distinction between linguistic fluency and innate creativity – the latter is blankness/nothingness in the absence of rules and structure, whereas the former entails being able to play within the existing rules of a language.

Our ability to catch subtleties in the language grows in school, as every child brings in their own unique family languages from their households; the words and phrases that they habitually utter. Initially, we need a bit of getting accustomed to these home dialects, but we eventually come to grasp the various ways of tweaking the language without interfering in the conveyance of the essential meaning; often, this leads to changes in the language or the invention of new language items within the community. All of these, however, occur within the foundation of the structure we learned in our preschool years. Veering far from the conventions of the syntax will not only be unaccepted, but you will also be treated as an outsider.

In any event, school life broadens the horizon of linguistic fluency, adding sophistication and richness to the extent of us being able to catch subtleties of the language. We are exposed to a vast array of social networks and academic subjects, in addition to everyday language, meaning that we compete to gain knowledge among our peers.

The rigid social system has paralysed our minds' linguistic creativity. People often ask, "Why do I feel as if I'm a different person when I speak another language?" That's because a language is a tool that is used in accord with the culture governing our behaviour, and every country has its own distinct culture that is realised through this system.

This led me to a hypothesis: if we could create a learning environment where we are free to act like a child, without the fear of being humiliated, it would be much easier for adults to acquire a second language! But, of course, we have a job – maybe multiple jobs. We have responsibilities. So, this is where flexible and resilient people (or those with child-like minds) have an advantage, seemingly able to tap into the psyche of a child at will, or to hypnotise themselves into getting psyched up for success, with no fear of failure.

Fear of Making Mistakes

In school, we also learned the pain of making mistakes and being embarrassed in front of others, through which we developed a fear of failure and uncertainty. Consequently, we have learned to play it safe by avoiding potential challenges and risks. Some of us, however, learn to enjoy the thrill of venturing into the unknown, taking risks. These individual behavioural differences between us are largely dictated by our upbringings and by the people who influenced us in the early stages of mental development. Our past experiences, particularly those that shaped our personality traits, have been stored in our long-term memory, protecting us like guardians angels. The most unforgettable memories are those that are associated with emotions; whether they are positive or negative, they have been firmly established in our brain, sending us warnings of danger or anything that could make us feel belittled, insecure, or miserable.

Memories of new events are prevented from forming or rewriting the brain; this mixing up of past and present memories associated with (good and bad) emotions influence our present behaviour. If the emotion tied to a certain event was negative, we would most likely try to avoid the same emotional experience in the future, as if believing that the same thing would occur. That way, we won't even give a second of thought to trying it again. Thus, the kind of emotions we store in our brain in association with past events will greatly influence the way we learn as adults and our levels of motivation and confidence. Will you let your past experiences dictate what you can and can't do?

Take a moment, and try to digest this. Our favourite songs from the past evoke certain emotions based on the events that took place when we were listening. The song may be about love or hate. It may be about break-ups, saying good-byes, or even about death. Each concept contains an emotion or two, so when you hear the song, it brings back the emotions you had attached to that particular event.

We do not have much control over the early stages of our lives, but, as adults, we can acknowledge the patterns, becoming aware of them when we start to learn a second language. It is not easy. We have to keep pushing ourselves, staying wary of those existing behaviour patterns that limit us at all times.

Memory and Emotions

What is critical to remember here is that emotions became attached or associated with these events while we were producing language, so the events most intensely associated with our emotions are the ones that we would have most difficulties forgetting. To this day, those positive or negative memories may have driven you forwards (if positive) or held you back (if negative).

To master a second language as an adult, we need to constantly work on developing the ability to reset these seemingly invincible memories; otherwise, our learning behaviour will be dictated by the emotions of our past.

In light of this understanding, we must make it a habit to constantly remind ourselves that our emotions play an effective and critical role in remembering language. In other words, we must make sure that we channel our emotions into learning language without letting our past memories get in the way.

Willingness to Go Through the Pain Once Again

It is difficult for adult language learners to be willing to re-experience their early stages of life, but in another language. It is more difficult because of our memories of past events acting as the force that dictates much of our behaviour. Because our ways of interpreting life have been so fixed, we are unwilling to undergo such a troublesome process once again, especially since acquiring even a single piece of language often requires reconceptualisation. So why bother with this rudimentary task again? We have already gone through it! Why should we have to adapt to a new environment when we feel out of place?

In contrast, none of that concerns children learning other languages. They are carefree of nearly everything, which makes them the best language learners.

Our conservative mentalities and attitudes may change if the community of our second language is willing to accept and help us the same way it would support a little child trying to learn his or her first language. The reality, however, is that we are grown ups; we can't disguise our physical features and we can't get younger. If we acted like a child, we would most definitely draw some confused stares. Not many people would be as forgiving as they would be for a little kid. We cannot expect some benevolent teacher to materialize out of nowhere, teaching us every piece of language, and present for every step of our journey. More importantly, who among us would be willing to endure the pain of being humiliated in public places every so often? Imagine feeling useless when ordering a coffee, pointing your finger at what you want, because you don't have the words for it. People behind you would give you a long, annoyed stare. If everyone in our second language community is willing to help us like they would their own children, however, the odds of acquiring fluency will definitely be increased.

All of these factors should be taken into consideration and critically evaluated over the course of second language acquisition. We won't beat ourselves up over our failures. In other words, we should develop the ability to critically assess our progress in the presence of the distracting factors of reality.

Up to this point, we have discussed how we're born with an innate inventiveness which gradually dies out as the dogmas of culture seep into our brains and we submit to the existing system. Although this helps us to digest the language as a whole, turning it into an integral part of us, we lose, at the same time, our innate inventiveness of language in exchange. We've also talked about how adults who are rebellious when it comes to their cultures can learn more easily in the initial stages of second language acquisition.

The first step to being fluent in a foreign language is to examine yourself and to observe if our old habits are roadblocks to learning another language.

Chapter 5

Where Are You?

If you are already an independent learner in other areas of your life, you should already know the importance of examining your current cognitive, physical, and financial states, as well as reflecting on your past experiences and associated memories.

Where am I going with this particular language?

Being overly realistic is the most ineffective way to start learning anything because the predictability of the outcome will eventually kill our motivation. Though it is natural that we would weigh the pros and cons of our current and prospective actions by considering our real-life circumstances and obligations, the analytic part of our brain will limit us to what is obviously possible, encouraging us to play safe. Safety, predictability, and stability are certainty our enemies since we mainly learn language through epiphany – aha moments.

Romanticise the ultimate goal in your mind.

Fantastical Vision

For many adults, the idea of learning something new begins with *fantasies;* for instance, a vision of being able to travel the world because of the language. *If the vision is strong and lasting, it will be the driving force* throughout the journey. The fantastical vision might not cut us a clear path to follow, but it will provide us with directions so that we will not fall off track. Find your own fantastical vision. We all have different fantasies.

Be Conscious of Temptations

To regain innate intuitiveness in our language learning, we must acknowledge that the reality that our priorities are different at different stages of our lives. We must be aware of what distracts and tempts us in our immediate surroundings. *Examine distractions* and *temptations* in your daily life. Most adult males, for instance, are easily tempted by seductive materials and chemical stimulants that could fulfil their physiological needs – reproduction for the former and substance dependency for the latter. Small children in the critical period of physical and mental development do not have such needs. Most adult males subconsciously prioritise their acts to achieve three things: reproduction and improved financial and social statuses. Most children learning their first languages have none of these desires. They *learn language out of pure curiosity* and for *survival.* We should recognise the difference and be conscious of the distractions that hinder our progress.

Many popular social media language "gurus" suggest that we must "relax" when we learn a second language, but how can you relax when you have urgent physiological desires?

That is something you should figure out on your own.

Obligations

One critical distinction between adults and children is that children learn languages to survive and function in society, abilities that most adults already have. Our life obligations and duties to ourselves and our families are major drawbacks that *suppress our innate creativity and ultimately prevent us from accessing the unlimited realm of possibility.*

Second Language Above Anything

To acquire another language, the value of doing so should be your goal above anything else. I urge you to carefully look into all the aspects of your current life to see if your *living situation* or *environment* is conducive to achieving your goal. If the circumstances are not in your favour, you must make changes.

So... can you?

Chapter 6

Turn Your Memories of the Past into Lexis and Syntax

How many times have you cried in your first language?

How many times have you screamed
or yelled at someone or yourself in your first language?

How many times have you lost your mind
and got pissed at somebody in your first language?

How many times have you been frustrated
with someone because of miscommunication?

How many times have you failed and been disappointed in your life?

How many compelling relationships have you had,
and why are you unable to forget about them?

How many friends and acquittances have you
made who speak your first language?

How many songs lyrics can you recall in your first language?

How emotionally attached are you
to all of those memories in your first language?

Our first language learning environment was context-rich. The frustrations of going from babbling to uttering the first word, running around with toys in your hands on the playground, roleplaying with other kids, learning to discuss in groups in elementary school, getting bullied in middle school, and then learning to fight back in high school, going through puberty, and having sex for the first time. All of your *emotional and personal* experiences occurred in your first language.

Now, are we thinking about re-experiencing those enormous and laborious life events to evoke thousands of sensations through another language? Do we have to acquaint ourselves or deal with thousands of more good and bad people in another language?

No.

The Way We Remember Things

Take a step back and think for a second. When we recall information about past events, what do we get? Fragmented visuals, muffled sounds, and emotions? Except for some people with ingenious photographic memories, most of us recall information in the form of visuals, text, sounds, and smells – basically, the senses. And our brain translates the information into either text or sound to communicate. Now imagine.

What if you possessed all of the vocabulary in your second language that perfectly illustrates your past life experiences?

Do you think your brain could tell whether the events were experienced in your first language or second?

What you need to do is to play out the past events in your head, but in your second language, as if you were re-experiencing them in another language. Then, try to recall the memory of the event later. What does this conjure? Usually, the first things that occur without us realising are certain feelings of the event combined with whatever triggered our physical senses. And, if we were to talk about the event, we would have to translate an array of components of memory – words, phrases, and sentences – into language

This means that, if we have all of the pieces of language to illustrate our past life experiences in a second language, we don't have to re-experience them.

Only the Lexis and Syntax

Following this logic, all we need to do then is to find the language pieces that are interchangeable in meaning. If our second language does not have the lexis to describe our past experiences, we will have to invent a new word or use the ones that are closest in meaning in our second languages.

Now you have all of the vocabulary in your second language needed to illustrate your past life experiences. When someone asks you about your childhood, you can communicate the information in either your first or second language.

Once you have completely absorbed it in your mind, reaching the point of being able to receive and produce the language, you possess all of the words in your second language that are necessary to talk about your past experiences, but is it really enough?

Past Memory

1. Desire to communicate the information

2. Recall the past event

3. Bring back images, sounds, smells (sensory information)

4. Process the information either in the first or second language (subconscious level)

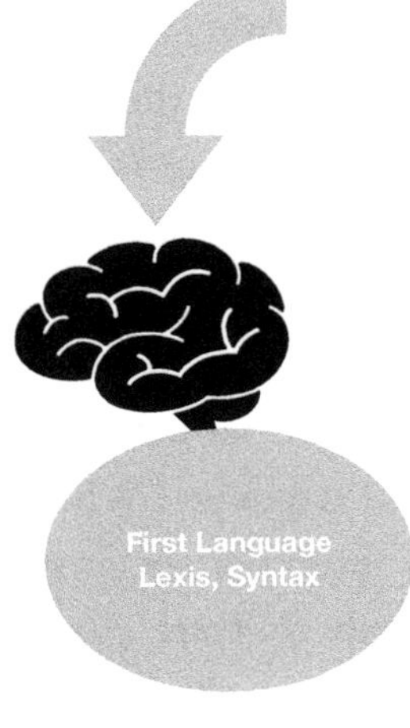

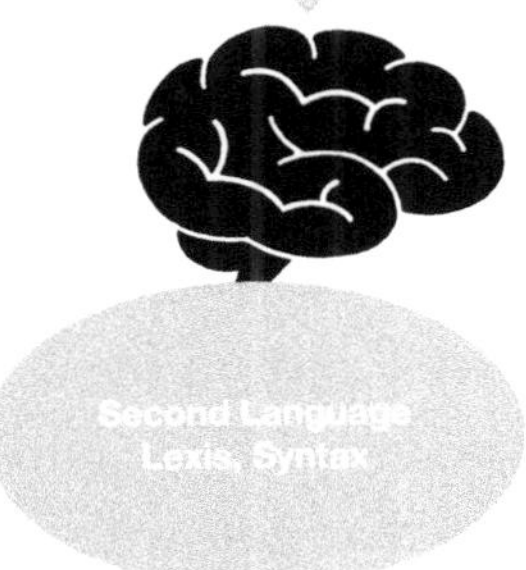

5. Communicate the information through text or sound

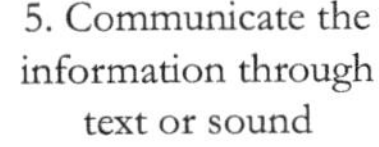

Cultural Perception and Conceptual Meaning

Suppose you are trying to learn the word "gang" in your second language. If the concept has the same connotation in your second language as in your first language, then you do not need to *experience* anything gang-related, because it is a shared concept in both cultures. If the meaning is interchangeable, all you need to do is learn its phonetic and textual elements. If the meaning is perceived and interpreted differently, however, you have to find a way to bridge the gap.

Interchangeability in Meaning

If you had a dark past, living as a gang member in a ghetto somewhere in Harlem, you would find it difficult to express the experience through another language, for instance, Korean. It simply means that the same experience cannot exist in Korean society; even if it does, it is not identical. For this reason, your second language is inadequate, as it cannot provide the lexis for your past experiences. You feel that your first language is the only language that can perfectly portray your past, and that no other languages can match.

We CANNOT achieve the same authenticity in another language. Why? Because you are trying to express something that does not exist in the culture of your second language. What you can do instead is *to find ways to describe* your experiences, which means that you will have to learn the words that are closest in meaning to that of your first language.

Now, given that we possess the vocabulary to do so, we can explain our past experiences with our second language.

That's not good enough, however, to acquire another language.

Chapter 7

Reinvent Your Past Experiences in Your Second Language

Follow these procedures if you would like to create another version of your past experiences in the context of your second language. You MUST trick and condition your brain to achieve this.

Procedures

Find source material – like a movie or TV show – that illustrates the concept, watch it, and study the differences.

STEP 1. Notice and Understand the Cultural Differences

Suppose you watch a Korean movie about school gangsters. You notice that they don't carry guns, nor do they wear sagging pants. The Korean language is then incapable of communicating some aspects of your past experiences as a gang member because it cannot achieve the authenticity of the real experience. In this case, you will have to learn the language pieces to explain the difference.

Providing additional information to explain your past experiences, however, is not enough to acquire your second language.

STEP 2. Condition Your Brain

Now, imagine as if you're actually in the scene, speaking Korean, but do not think that this is unreal or virtual. You must psych up your mind into believing that you actually live in that world. This works because, when you try to recall later, your brain does not know whether you've actually experienced it or not. It simply brings back the memory in sensory forms. If there is any difference in context or meaning, learn the difference and reinvent your past event as if you're experiencing it through another language in a different context. You wouldn't carry guns, nor would you wear sagging pants. Instead, you would wear a tight school uniform, with perfectly combed hair and maybe a bit of make up on your face, as some Korean boys do. As a result, when you try to recall your past experiences as a gang member, your brain will bring back two different versions of the event: one in your first language and one in your second.

STEP 3. Recall from Memory

Now, depending on to whom you are talking and in what context you'd like to communicate, your brain will retrieve the information from either version of the story. You have two versions of the event, one that you actually experienced in your original culture and one existing in your imagination in the second language's culture. Think for a second. How does your brain recall information about the event? Can it recognise the difference between one that you have actually experienced and one that you have imagined as if you experienced it?

Only you can tell which is real and which is fake. What your brain brings back are simply *different forms of memory: visual, auditory, textual, haptic,* and *emotional.*

STEP 4. Build Vocal Muscles Until They Are on Autopilot

Whether your first language and second share many cultural elements or not, the production of new sounds requires new vocal muscles to grow. The reality is that the muscles in adults' vocal cords and diaphragms, the parts in the body that control and produce sound development until the age of 30. In these particular areas of the body, you are obviously not an infant, but your vocal frame is strong enough to produce sounds. It is just so rigid. For this reason, we first need to *familiarise* ourselves with the sounds that we'd like to understand and produce until doing so is no longer laborious.

DIFFICULTY

On a biological and genetic level, the vocal muscle groups used for the production of sounds are shaped primarily for the purpose of speaking your first language. Think of it as body-building. If you develop only one particular muscle group, while neglecting others, only that part will receive the benefits of the development. In exchange, other muscle groups will regress.

So, we have to *intentionally loosen up our first language muscles* and *reshape them.*

How long does it take for newborn babies to utter their first words in their first languages? For most babies, it takes up to *14 months*. They can't do it earlier because they just don't have all the muscles to produce all the sounds. Producing sound is easy for adults, but the problem lies in the fact that adult vocal systems have been optimised to function for only one language.

SOLUTION

Now, every time you hear a letter, word, or sentence in your second language, you must trick your mind into believing that you have never heard anything similar in your first language. Take in the word as it sounds. Do not try to find a similar sound in your first language to match it. Maybe it's easier for you to understand if I told you that people tend to speak a bit more fluently when they're a bit tipsy. Why? Because they do not overthink. They do not give themselves the time to try to derive sounds from memories of their first languages' sounds. They are in the moment.

Start babbling.

Chapter 8

Our Difficulties with Vocabulary

Reality of Adult Vocabulary

Ask yourself this question: How many words do you know in your first language? I want you to pause and think for a moment. If you are an adult like me, you have acquired a vocabulary of 30,000 to 42,000 words in your first language (see the graph below).

How Many Words?

This graph indicates the number of vocabulary words acquired at different ages. A mere 50 words are recognisable in the first year after birth. By age three, the total adds up to 1,000 words. Four year olds know about 5,000 words, and, at about five, another 10,000 words. Most eight year olds know slightly above 15,000 words. Does this mean that they would just suck vocabulary up like a vacuum cleaner? Effortlessly? Absolutely not.

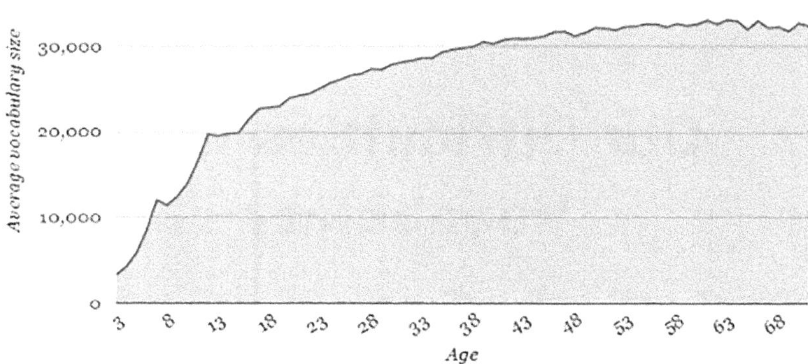

LIFE STAGES

Newborn
a baby that was just born

Baby
from birth to 1 year old

Toddler
between 12 months and 2-3 years old.

Child
someone younger than a teenager

Pre-teen
10–12 years old

Teenager
13–19 years old

Adult
over the age of 19

Elderly
60+ years old

Linguistics Elements

There is a certain set of vocabulary for each age group. When you are in kindergarten, you learn the language needed to function as a little boy or girl. Most of the language you speak is simple and straightforward. When you are a teen, you use lots of slang and trendy words among your peers.

Maybe, in your 30s, you might want to focus on learning the language for your particular age group or the one to which you're most exposed, for instance, the common language at your work place. Some of you may be more ambitious, targeting more than one age group, like language for both young adults and middle age. You may be keen on using the language of your culture's aristocrats or for well-educated people. Just as with the English language, every language has a variety of dialects, accents, and classes, and the time it takes to acquire the language will depend on the number of age groups you've selected – the more groups, the longer. Additionally, the more sophisticated and intellectual the language of your chosen age group, the longer it will take for you to master that specific language. I'd suggest that it is important to be realistic, setting attainable goals that you can follow through everyday.

For instance, imagine you are a teenager trying to reach the level of fluency of a teenager in your second language. You would have to retain the amount of vocabulary (20,000) that average teenagers possess. You would also have to understand the meanings of common phrases, norms, and trends that are associated with the language. These are the components of language that are subconsciously running through the minds of your counterparts, controlling their behaviour. If you and them have many overlapping cultural elements in this aspect of language, it will take much less time than those who you feel to be culturally remote from you. For most Koreans, it is a lot easier to learn Chinese than French, because all they have to do is to learn the linguistic features of the language – such as pronunciation and vocabulary – since their cultures share many aspects of life.

Cultural Elements

If your culture and the culture of your second language are essentially different, the acquisition will take longer. You always have a choice of whether to try understanding the cultural differences associated with the language items or to ignore them, only paying attention to the mechanics of the language. In that case, you may look seemingly proficient on a verbal level, but you won't be able to integrate the emotions and connotations that are associated with the language.

The cost of not trying hard to understand cultural aspects that are associated with the language is that you would not be able to identify yourself with the language. It will always be foreign to you. You will easily forget about the language if you don't use it often, proving unable to integrate the language into your life. Language learnt this way will – most likely – be the kind of language that sounds mechanical and emotionless.

You may argue that you are able to process information in your second language as quickly and accurately as native speakers, but, without the establishment of another identity in the language, the language you produce is only derived from rote memorisation, which has only been processed cognitively. You may know all the words and have no difficulties receiving and producing information, but your proficiency only exists on a word-to-word basis.

Acquisition requires emotional experiences, and these experiences form memories through which you identify yourself.

Reality Check and Action Plan:

Let's say you have amassed a large vocabulary in your second language, and you understand the cultural norms of the particular age group you selected. If your initial goal was to acquire the language of people in their 30s, but you don't possess the languages spoken among the other age groups that weren't your focus, you have skipped learning their languages. That is only natural, because you can only understand things within the range of language you've covered and acquired. You just need to relax and carry on, continuing to learn the language of your target age group; when you feel that you've reached the level of mastery of that group's language, you can expand your horizon over to other age groups. Eventually, you will be able to understand children, teen, and adult language.

Vocabulary from Loved Ones

As a child learning your first language, you have *sacrificial* parents who are willing to tirelessly repeat the same words, phrases, and expressions, stringing together short and long sentences especially for you, in conjunction with lots of *contextual explanations*. Most importantly, they do this *with love*, hoping to see you *grow*.

In addition, children have *peers* from school or any other *social activities* where everyone can bring in the lexis used in their specific households. This *interpersonal interaction* gives them the chance to learn a variety of accents, dialects, and expressions.

As adults, we have none of the kind of support and interaction a child would have.

Our Alternatives as Adult Language Learners

We have to find ways to simulate the same kind of environment a child has, whether it be through our imagination or by living in the country where our second language is spoken.

Alternative One: *Find someone who loves to talk to you. It could be friends, co-workers, or anyone who enjoys talking to you about a wide array of interesting subjects.*

Alternative Two: *Find and watch lots of interesting TV shows or movies where actors engage in a variety of conversations, and imagine you are in the scene.*

Where Are You Heading?

To begin your journey, you need to select a specific age group to which all of your attention will be paid.

My original goal was to learn the language that covers the time from birth to my age, 25, but I soon realised it was practically impossible to keep track of my progress on such a large scale. I *narrowed it down specifically to my age group* first, and then aimed at the kind of vocabulary that was most frequently used by people around my age. Lacking an attainable goal will kill your motivation. Although the outcome doesn't have to be crystal clear or predictable, you must know the basic direction in which you're heading; otherwise, you will keep making comparisons and beating yourself up over things that you don't know or that you lack at the moment.

Examine Your Living Environment

We have to create our own learning environments, and I fear that I can't really help you much there, as we live in different places and our circumstances vary. I trust, however, that you will learn far more and faster if you become your own educational designer. In the context of acquiring a second language, this means that you should learn to design a child's language learning environment by reshaping your current environment. It is truly powerful how our immediate surroundings can change the way we perceive things.

For instance, I was in college when I decided to learn English. Obviously, the kind of language I would encounter throughout most of my days was mainly academic. Being in college, I would spend most of my day reading academic articles and textbooks, as well as doing campus related activities. I would've been a fool if I'd tried to change the circumstances to learn another language than what I was being naturally exposed to. I tried to acquire as much vocabulary as an average native speaker university student possesses, but I couldn't understand if a child said 'bunny' to me instead of 'rabbit.'

Understanding our individual circumstances, you are the only one who can come up with actionable plan.

What needs to be done? Observe and find ways to break through.

If we had enough vocabulary to cover all the age groups of our second language, would it mean that we have achieved native-like fluency?

We will discuss this in later chapters.

Chapter 9

Learn the Way You Learn

Now that you *have selected a specific age group* or have found a specific focus, you may be asking, 'Where to look to execute my plan?'

Language acquisition is different from learning subjects in school. I remember that all I did during my school years was merely kill time in the back of the classroom and that my favourite food was cigarettes. I detested rote memorisation, as I felt that it was not an effective way to learn. Language acquisition does NOT occur by simply repeating the same thing.

Vacuum State

Your mind has to be in a state of vacuum, wide open to receive information and integrate the material into the entirety of your mind. In other words, the language learning process must involve *experience* and *emotion,* and then *internalisation* of the memories into our *subconscious minds*.

The subject of second language learning has to be treated differently than a subject like astronomy, in which one cannot physically experience much of the subject matter (Mars, Jupiter).

The most effective way of learning is *experiential, since it triggers all of our senses.* We must find ways to experience events with the intent of *stimulating our senses.* The language learnt in this manner is difficult to forget, as memory of the event is associated with emotion. When the language is stored in our mind in this manner, it becomes an *integral* part of our way of thinking. After this initial framework is set in place, the rest is like learning a new sport, requiring countless repetition.

Mindful Repetition in Second Language Learning

Repetition, whether it is spaced out or not, is only useful for testing knowledge. To integrate a piece of language into your mind, your senses must be triggered, so that you are *mindfully-engaged* in the language. Every time you utter a word, it requires your *physical capabilities, mental and cognitive power,* and *cultural, social, and ideological understanding of the word's culture.* Repetition is essential only if carried out in the presence of those elements. You will experience and realise that the internalisation and integration of language in the mind require far more than mindless repetition. They require the kind of repetition that focuses attention on our emotions concerning what's happening at the moment.

Living Being

You will then see the language as a *living being.* It's not just text that informs us. It is around us and alive at all times. Once you realise this, you will start wondering about the names of things in your second language's environment, coming to love its dynamics.

Your Are the Performer

The process of acquiring another language is much like taking up a new sport – you become the performer, not the coach. You don't study the language for the purpose of becoming a spectator. A coach has a great deal of knowledge about the sport, but it's the athlete who will have to play on the field. Remember that you are the performer of the language you're learning.

I Know NOTHING About Life Mindset

When we were little, we tried to experience many different things in our surroundings because we were curious. Our *curiosity* is triggered, and we get to experiment the unknown. Once we realise that it is safe to play with it, despite some initial *difficulties*, we will seek more and repeat the process. If the experience is *continuously* and *consistently pleasant*, we will develop *a long-term* fondness and may practice it for the rest of our lives. If the experience is unpleasant, or if it inflicts an *unbearable* degree of mental or physical pain, we will quit and won't dare try again. Consequently, we learn the meaning of pain. This is what we must first overcome.

As an adult language learner, you don't have the luxury of being a curious child. Most of your actions toward learning are *voluntary, intentional, and conscious, as your actions are dictated by your past memories.* As your past memories remind you of those painfully emotional experiences, you subconsciously put up your guard to protect yourself from experiencing pain when you try to learn something new.

To regain innate intuitiveness (neuro-plasticity, creativity), we must learn to prevent those past memories from entering our minds.

You must psych yourself up to engender the sensations of burning necessity and curiosity needed to absorb another language as a whole. In such a mental state, you can't help being so careless about making mistakes or losing face in public places. You won't care whether you sound like a mentally-stunted child speaking an alien language.

What resources do you have? Is it your social personality allowing you to easily make *friends* anywhere? You may be somebody who is naturally insensitive, or, perhaps, you are immune to feeling a sense of shame at what may be, for most adults, public humiliation. Are you an introvert to the point that it allows you to learn most effectively via computer software within the confines of your own room? If you are the former, a good starting point will be getting out to *socialise*. If you are the latter, *learn to read first*.

In other words, you must first learn about your learning style, during which you will learn so much about your nature, uncovering who you truly are as a learner. Do not let any of those popular language programs or computer softwares fool your rational mind if you don't feel right for you. *Experiment with various tools, aids, or instructors, employing the ones that work for you.*

Again, it will take some time to *learn the way you learn* things.

Chapter 10

Necessity vs. Curiosity

Are you in a position or place where your survival and success in society depend on how successfully you integrate your second language?

You may have started out as an immigrant or, perhaps, a refugee. Even after 20 years of residency, you cannot speak the language properly. In reality, you've never had the willingness fully integrate into the society. You smirk at the idea of ditching your old habits and abandoning your traditions. The idea of adopting a new culture and language makes you cringe. You believe that you are doing absolutely fine within the confines of your own community because you feel *content*. As a result, you refuse to experience the discomfort and ambiguity of living life in your second language. You cannot bear the humiliation of not knowing how to express yourself or, for that matter, losing face. The real problem, however, is that you don't even know the origin of these feelings. You believe that it is natural for you to feel this way, when, in fact, your feelings come from your past memories that you used in developing an identity. As a result, you stick to the tiny community of your fellow countrymen.

I'd say that, if you're happy in there, stay put. If you feel a burning desire deep inside of you and have the willingness to learn more about the world, get the hell out.

Difference

Learning begins with making a distinction between *necessity* and *curiosity*. Necessity is connected to survival, whereas curiosity is linked to amusement, each of which is a powerful motivational factor.

As adults with fully-developed brains, we can easily find a way around seemingly helpless situations. We lie to ourselves to avoid learning the hard way, refraining from becoming cunning in the face of difficulties, instead turning back to our comfort zones. Even in remote places in foreign countries, if we try to locate our fellow countrymen, we can do so easily. It is so hard to put ourselves in a desperate situation where we are forced or obliged to learn a language such that our survival will be on the line if we don't. Even many of those refugees find ways to survive in their host countries without having to learn their languages properly. If there is a way around, then why bother? For this reason, our major motivational factor should be *curiosity*.

Learning Out of Curiosity

Curiosity beats necessity.

You are not dumb. If you think hard enough, you will find a way to ensure a pleasant experience in picking up another language. There are no rules as to how to acquire the language, as our various living conditions and adult obligations dictate our day-to-day schedule. For this reason, I suspect that no one can come up with an optimal learning schedule for you. You must be autonomous in this. Figure out the amount of free time you have, the resources available to you, and the opportunities for linguistic and cultural immersion.

Chapter 11

Grown-Ups' Advantages

"You cannot defeat those who enjoy doing."

Going against or becoming too detached from the norm can often lead to *isolation* and *humiliation*. This thought is *deeply embedded* in our minds on a subconscious level – so much so that it prevents us from trying new things like learning a language. We know that trying something new will most likely bring amp feelings of insecurity, shame, invalidation, or uncertainty. Humiliating mistakes make us feel patronised and belittled.

When we were little and learning our first language, people were much more forgiving and kinder because we were children and they understood our struggles. If a grown-up, however, speaks in public using only the most basic language, barely making sense to others, many people will grimace, cringe, or ignore them. So our natural inclination is to avoid those situations. This is a good example of why adults are not perfect second language learners. Again, it's the memories of our past mistakes and embarrassments that accompany language learning. These memories that makes us hesitate before trying new things, overthinking the potential consequences of mistakes.

It is those memories that command you not to challenge yourself in real-life situations, keeping you in a safe, comfortable place, where we just turn to passive learning tools, like smartphone apps.

Are you an introvert?

Leverage the Adult Mind

Regularly remind yourself that you're always under the strains of society, which suppress the fluid mind of a child that still exists deep inside of you. Try to think back to what it was like to be a child. You will have some flashbacks associated with certain emotions. Think about the difference in mentality between you as a child and you now.

What are the main characteristics of children?

1. *Being irresponsible for their actions*
2. *Not fixating on the consequences of their actions or behaviour*
3. *Being unintentionally less logical in speech and writing*
4. *Making sense of things in their own rights*
5. *Having a strong resistance to boring activities*
6. *Being curious about nearly all things in life (until making the very first mistake)*
7. *Asking boundless questions*
8. *Being more willing to receive and accept help*
9. *Quickly adjusting or changing their needs*
10. *Being unwilling to reflect on their behaviour*

What are the main characteristics of an adult?

1. *Self-reflection*
2. *Organising information or sorting things out*
3. *Logical analysis, or a tendency to analyse*
4. *Favouring stability, certainty, predictability, familiarity, and repeated regular actions*
5. *Values discipline, self-restraint, and principles*
6. *Seeks moral high-grounds*
7. *Seeks self-validation*
8. *Seeks social acceptance*

Ability to Switch Back and Forth Between Child and Adult

There are some important traits of the adult mind that we often forget about, since most of our actions are done without question. Examine your own actions, and see what aspects of your personality give you an advantage over child language learners. For instance, *habitual and regular self-reflection* is one critical factor that differentiates an adult from a child, though too much contemplation can also prevent curiosity from firing up. It is a factor that requires many years to fully develop to the extent that an adult learner has an advantage.

Let's say you've had a conversation with a native speaker of your second language, and you realised you've made an error in your word choice, saying something incorrectly. If you're a child, you're most likely carefree when it comes to your mistakes and won't correct yourself independently unless someone – a parent or teacher – corrects you. As an adult language leaner, you need to take on both roles: a disciplined coach and a childlike learner.

Fluid Attitude

You will have to understand that there is no shame in making mistakes, as that's only natural while learning new things of any sort. Many adults shy away from learning anything new because, growing up, they learnt how it felt to be humiliated by their mistakes, which has an impact on an emotional level. You won't be able to become fluent in any language or in any skills if you do not overcome that attitude. Let me say that again: you won't achieve anything in life with that attitude.

To get started is to *eliminate the fear of trying something unfamiliar* that pressures you so much. You might have the urge to *learn to speak first* when you don't even realise that you hate talking, when you are already so awkward in social settings in your first language. In this case, what you are trying to do is not only learn another language, but to also push yourself to develop a persona that is radically different from your persona in your mother tongue. In its essence, you are, in fact, looking at personality transformation.

A *Stick to your old ways of learning (with no personality transformation)*

or

B *Transform yourself to learn another language by developing new learning habits*

Reality

You are not a child, which means you aren't in the critical period when your personality is forming and your brain is most malleable. Your concepts of the world aren't vague anymore; as an adult, your thoughts have been hard-wired, whether consciously or unconsciously, in the cultural and political ideologies passed down for generations – deeply embedded in your brain cells and genes. As a consequence, your way of thinking and your worldly knowledge undoubtedly limit your language-learning capabilities, because the language is culturally, politically, and ideologically so different from your first language. If you grew up in a Confucian-based society, you will find it much more difficult to learn a European language, but will surely find it easy to learn the languages from the countries that share many linguistics features due to their shared belief system.

Fossilised Brain

With our fossilised brains, changing the whole structure of our mind and regenerating the cells needed to learn another language seems infeasible. Like how the 20+ years you've been afraid of public speaking won't change overnight simply because you're motivated. For some of you, the idea of learning another language might sound intriguing, possibly providing you with the opportunity to push yourself out of your comfort zone and reshape your personality. Maybe this is why some of the best adult language learners are those who detest their culture, their first language, their personality, or their persona in their culture. They wanted a radical change and picked up another language that reflected a culture radically different from their own.

Let's be frank. Our habits have been developed over the years, so changes can only occur gradually. If the manner in which changes occur is abrupt or too imposing on yourself, it may have a traumatic impact on your mental health. Shocked, your first self will bounce back up. Having an identity crisis is one example where you experience an inferiority complex, feeling inadequate; you feel invalidated in your living community. But, then again, if you are bold enough to deflect those feelings, or if you're immune to public embarrassment, not caring about the idea of social status, all of that won't matter, *because you are like a child, seeing things as if you were seeing them for the first time and willing to learn anything about the language.* You live in the absence of biases, stereotypes, and prejudices.

Interaction

You may have to reshape your personality to learn to speak another language because it will often require you to talk to strangers (and to be comfortable doing so). If you enjoy that, you may be able to learn the language. Interactions with strangers from another country *reinforces* you, helping you take great pleasure in communicating with people from different parts of the world. Bits of language you've exchanged over the years become sorted and integrated into your system. Just remember, though, that developing a new persona takes time and its formation occurs gradually.

Retain Good Qualities of Your First Language

With an open mind comes the willingness to adopt new habits and ways of living, which will eventually lead to forming the new personas and attitudes required for full integration of another language into your existing system. This does not mean you have to abandon your earlier language traits; you should retain some of the GOOD qualities of your first language. In this way, it is not so much discarding the entirety of your first language, but rather developing a full awareness of the cultural, linguistic, and ideological differences between your first and second. Some may argue that complete immersive learning is the most effective way to learn another language. Perhaps. But that's also a sure way to confuse your identity. If you already have a strong mind and mental endurance to make it through the pain of an identity crisis, you can go ahead and dive headfirst into the culture of your target language. In time, you will eventually realise you don't belong there. You will realise that you've been away from the country of your first language for too long. That's when you will realise that you don't belong in either place.

So, for starters, discover the advantages of being an adult language learner by examining yourself and slowly stepping out of the confines.

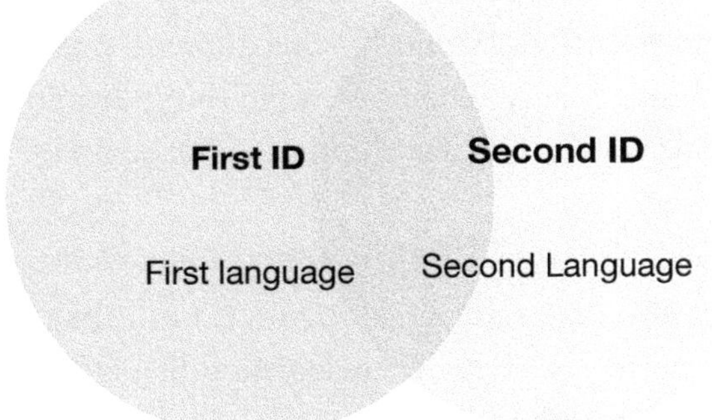

Chapter 12

From Nothing to Standard

Learning a second language is like picking up a new sport. Initially, we're all careful observers, and only few of us become the doers. You watch professional athletes' performances and enjoy their moves, but you can learn only few on your own.

Curiosity —> Dare —> Exposure

For adult language learners, when something grabs their attention, they need to then *pay full attention to it,* whether it's a person or a thing. Then they'll decide whether they'd like to let it hold their attention. We do this because we put up a shield of protection immediately when a strange thing or person enters our consciousness. We become cautious and begin to measure possi-ble risks.

Children are different. If they spot things that grab their attention, they will dive right in, enjoying it until they get bored. These early experiences shape their learning behaviour and attitude later in their adulthoods.

As an adult, most situations come down to either fight or flight, and language learning is no different. As adult language learners, there is a degree of fear of the unknown, greater than it was when we were children, since we've already experienced what it's like to fail and grow disappointed with things we once deeply cared about learning. Solution?

1. Study the patterns of your learning behaviour as an adult, and see if you feel that it's been holding you back from being curious or daring to try new things.
2. Track down the source of your fear. Think back to the learning experiences of your childhood, asking the following questions: were there any past events that have had a negative impact on your learning attitude as an adult? If so, is that particular experience making you fear trying new things and taking risks?
3. Once you figure out the answers to 1 and 2, try to expose yourself to the source of your fears, one at a time. Gradually increase the frequency of contact with your fears.

For instance, you may want to open a bank account in a foreign country, but you fear the possibility of being humiliated in front of people. That's the tendency most adults have when they're about to face a challenge, measuring the consequences or impacts of our actions. That's because they have experienced the feelings of humiliation many times to the extent that they've conceptualised the fear of failure. Such a preconceived notion is our most formidable enemy, as it prevents us from taking proactive steps forward, hampering our progress as well. Therefore, in the initial stage of learning a second language, we DON'T think like that. We must fool our minds, psyching them up to think that we are incapable of calibrating the pros and cos of our actions. Only then will we DARE try anything.

Self-reflection must come later.

Action Plan One: Your Mind

Prejudice and Judgement

Ask yourself this question: do you remember how you learned things when you were a little? Deep down, we know what sparks the initial step – CURIOSITY. This is curiosity in the absence of prejudice, judgement, bias, and precedence. *Being curious* leads us to take the first step towards whatever intrigues us. It starts with a feeling of *half fear* and *half thrill*. Overcoming the former, we must let the latter take control of the engine, propelling us in the direction of where we *wish* to be. Either intentionally and unintentionally, we get more exposure to the thing, learning about it until we understand it. As the frequency of contact increases, so does our understanding and familiarity with whatever we're trying to learn.

Again, remind yourself at this stage that *prejudice and judgement have no place* in second language leaning. You do not have *preconceptions* or *preconceived notions* about the language and culture.

Your mind is like a child's, ready to devour all input from any sources of information. You're not thinking about how you'll remember everything. You just listen, giving it your full attention without judging, trying to understand about what's going on in the current situation.

You will *unconditionally* and *blindly* accept what you hear or read. As adults, a lot of us can just barely remember the sense of complete innocence and purity we used to have when we were little. As adults, we can't quite regain that state of mind, primarily because, over the years, we have developed the habit of comparing and judging every new thing based on our past experiences or precedents. Instead of trying to absorb our second language in its entirety, automatically accepting its authenticity, we judge and compare it with our own.

Change the Way You Think of Mistakes

Babies do not understand the concept of making a mistake because they *haven't conceived* or *conceptualised* it in their minds. A mistake becomes a mistake only when we accept it as one, allowing it to negativity affect our emotional state. From then on, a fear of mistakes develops in our minds and we become increasingly conscious of the consequences of making a mistake. The problem is that fear sometimes makes our minds incapable of knowing if feelings are coming from a life-threatening danger or something simply unknown to us. These strong feelings of fear are derived from the memories of our past mistakes.

Self-Reflection

As an adult language learner, you cannot undo your past mistakes, but you can study their impact on your current habits and state of mind, becoming aware of how those old memories can influence your desire to learn. This ability to reflect on your life and yourself is critical for adults to learn anything – and it's one of the few areas where we are better than children. So use it when necessary, while remembering not to let it turn into overanalysis or overthinking.

Action Plan Two: Your Body

Exposure and Curiosity

We may seem mentally challenged if we act like a little child, running around in a restaurant, but, in the initial stage of learning a second language, we have to learn to embrace many awkward and embarrassing situations, accepting the fact that we may look like a silly, nonsensical kid. You can always reflect on your mistakes later, but, when you're in the moment, just be in the moment.

When you have fully regained the ability to be like a child, you will notice a few things inside of you:

- A burning curiosity and willingness to accept the new norms
- A high level of tolerance for the unknown
- Thick skin to handle the pressure of any language learning environment
- The ability to handle ignorant people who might jump to conclusions about you

Exposure —> Curiosity —> Voluntary Participation —> Familiarisation —> Understanding

A curious child whose mind has no concept of making a mistake, also does not know much about thinking things through, planning, or analysing and reflecting on past experiences. Children will let curiosity dominate their minds.

Some children have more curiosity than others, to the extent that it completely overrides their fear, leading to more exposure, whether they're dealing with a tangible, physical matter or an abstract idea.

Whatever it is that draws our attention, it has to be placed in *proximity* to us or it must be *novel*. In addition, to make it easier for us to be curious about it, we must *minimise* the amount of distractions in our living environment, focusing only on the one thing that makes us curious.

When curiosity compels our minds, prompting us to take gingerly steps forward, moving us, inch by inch, towards the thing that interests us, we start observing its physical features and mechanisms, until we come to a conclusion that it won't pose any life-threatening danger. By this point, someone comes onto the scene to demonstrate what to make of it; we watch the person enjoying the thing – a *model* for what we should do – and entertain the possibility that we might give it try. As this situation becomes a more regular occasion, its strangeness gradually wears off. When we reach that point, we start looking forward to the thing, because the whole learning environment has become a place that evokes the sense of *thrill,* not fear. Over time, *we develop a fondness* for the activity. We begin to make *meticulous observations to understand* every bit of its *mechanisms* and, most importantly, its *applications in real life*.

No Exposure —> No Curiosity

If we are not exposed to anything, there will never be anything to learn at all. At first, what we try to learn seems strange, but it is that *strangeness* that triggers our curiosity.

Fear

If a strange thing scares you away, you've got a problem, and that fear must be derived from your past experiences. Fix that first.

Desire to Imitate

What propels us to imitate the speakers of our second language? When causes us to be more willing to imitate the collective behaviours of our second language community?

1. Genuine Curiosity, Willingness to Experience Novelty, Passion for Learning
2. Willingness or Desperation for Acceptance
3. Seeking Self-Validation
4. Seeking a Sense of Belonging
5. Opportunities to Escape from First Language, Culture, or Society
6. Idolisation or Glorification of the Second Language Community
7. Inferiority Complex of Original Culture and Social Status
8. Insecurity of Self and/or Status

Stick to Number 1.

I have gone through those phases. Fortunately, I am now at 1, where my curiosity and passion keep me moving forward. Whatever reason you may have, there will come a point when understanding the language and watching people using the language are not good enough to *satisfy your passion* for the language. The *desire* to apply your knowledge to real life will prompt you to imitate and copy the fluent speakers of your second language. You more carefully watch them string words together and produce sounds, noticing how they respond to one another. You *do not analyse or criticise*. You just *receive*.

Then, there comes a point where your crave for knowledge *shifts from reception to production.* Unlike receiving information, however, producing takes more mental and physical power. It's not easy. That's because, so far, you've mainly been receiving, and, when you learn the difference in difficulty between receiving and producing, you'll likely get frustrated. It's not what you thought it would be. You had no problem understanding the language, so it should have been easy to speak, right? *If you've already forgotten why this is the case, go back to Chapter 5 and read through to Chapter 10 again.*

The degree to which you will continue to learn despite difficulties is determined by the language's degree of applicability and practicality to everyday life – does the *use of the language help you in some way?*

Find the Right Examples

To achieve the same effect as your first language's learning environment, you must intentionally put yourself in situations that *simulate that environment.* If that's realistically impossible, then you must learn to ***employ imagination*** (Chapter 5 to 10) in learning the language.

With the urge to imitate, you start your search for more extensive exposure to a variety of language pieces. You will not have as many opportunities as children learning their first languages, as they are exposed to various input sources like friends, parents, parents' friends, teachers, and strangers in random everyday places.

Standard Fluency (Average), What is Next?

Many years of diverse experiences in your second language will substantially increase your fluency, until you eventually reach a standard level of fluency. When you get there, you will get a strong feeling that you have been accepted, becoming part of the language community. You will feel that you've mastered not only the linguistic codes, but the cultural codes as well, and the collective behaviour shared within the community.

If you have reached this level, it most likely means that your first and second languages have reached the point of equilibrium.

Some of us, however, may not feel content; we may feel that we have plateaued with this standard level of fluency that literally everyone around us can demonstrate. Some of us may decide to step out of the pool in order to discover something that will distinguish us, something that will separate us from the rest of the crowd, through which we express our individuality.

From this point on, it's more about specialising in a specific field in which you will develop expertise.

Some Stay Put

Of course, not every one of us will have the ambition to become an expert of some sort, whether it's carried out in our first or second language. If you are content with the standard level of proficiency, you may as well stay there, remaining average, spending the rest of your life listening to others' input far more than you speak for yourself with your own confident language skills.

Journey of Acquisition

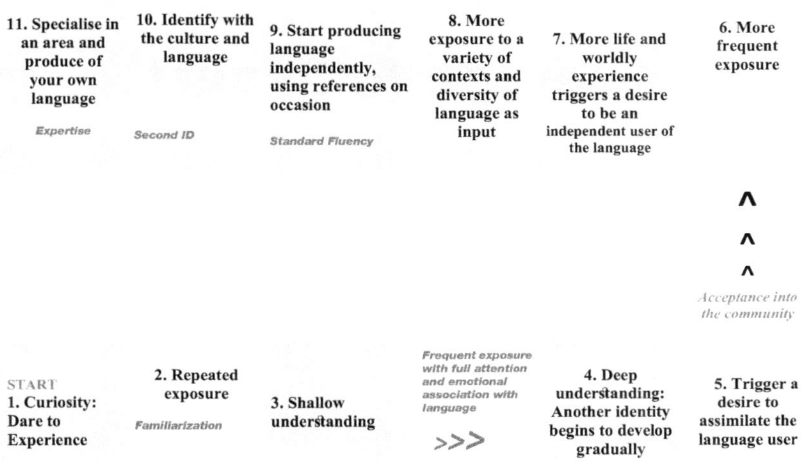

11. Specialise in an area and produce of your own language

Expertise

10. Identify with the culture and language

Second ID

9. Start producing language independently, using references on occasion

Standard Fluency

8. More exposure to a variety of contexts and diversity of language as input

7. More life and worldly experience triggers a desire to be an independent user of the language

6. More frequent exposure

^

^

^

Acceptance into the community

START

1. Curiosity: Dare to Experience

2. Repeated exposure

Familiarization

3. Shallow understanding

Frequent exposure with full attention and emotional association with language

>>>

4. Deep understanding: Another identity begins to develop gradually

5. Trigger a desire to assimilate the language user

Chapter 13

Average to Expert

Now that you've reached the level of standard fluency and you have no difficulties in receiving, understanding, and producing language in regards to nearly all matters of life, you feel that you've become part of the community and that you have established another identify amongst the people within the particular environment. Your second language community can be a country, a small community, online or offline – wherever it is, you will have a strong sense of attachment to it.

From this point onwards, you won't be able to survive just because you're fluent in another language; take a look around and notice that everyone is able to speak the language as fluently as you, so now you must begin to look for ways to contribute to the community or city. In other words, your standard fluency is not good enough to survive on. Some choose to become a translator or interpreter of some sort, while others choose a profession that requires vocational language with special terminologies used in the industries. It doesn't matter whether you're more fluent than a native speaker or not, in the end, you need to do something with the languages you speak.

Now, pause a moment.

Do you think the size of your vocabulary in your first language is as large as that of a lawyer, a sociology professor, or a doctor? If you are an average person with an average job without any particular occupational specialties, the size of your vocabulary is mostly related to mundane, everyday activities that are only good for surviving or doing manual labour.

To Become an Expert

Think of a living organism, a tree, for instance. When was your first time seeing one? How did you perceive it at first glance? Were there other living creatures, like a bunch of birds that had happened to perch on a branch of the tree while chirping on a clear sunny day in your hometown? You may have said to your mom, "This is so big! So tall! Wow!" and your mom may have responded in a loving teacherly voice, "Oh, sweetheart, it's a tree. They're good friends with us and with birds as well. Do you see those birds perched up top? They are very good friends with trees, making homes in them and living up there." Your eyes still full of curiosity, you may have asked, "So trees help birds?" and your mom would have gone a bit further, "Yes, trees help birds and they also help us by producing oxygen for us, which is the air we breathe." You go on to ask several more questions until your mom's too tired, making an excuse to stop.

Now, back to reality, could we possibly meet or hire an instructor with a willingness anywhere near as great as your mom's?

At this stage of learning, you have *understood* word and *associated* words (birds, singing, branches, big, perched, oxygen, air, breathe). The second time you came across a tree, you would be reminded of the things that your mom had said in her explanations. Not quite vividly, but clear enough to *conjure up images* of those objects and their concepts. But again, who would be willing to treat you like a baby learning the word "tree"? You're obviously a grown up.

The third time you saw the tree, you may have been without your mom, but with someone else, maybe friends from school. That day, you were supposed to plant a couple of trees together. Now, you have associated the memory of your friends with the act of planting trees, thereby forming a network connecting friends and the act of planting.

Your experience with living objects becomes *richer* with age, and, with more *frequent exposure, routine,* and *deliberate practice*, what was once merely a word gradually becomes a *solid foundation* from which your expert skills develop and expand.

You have seen trees in *visual* form. You have seen *many* species of them, and other *variables*. You have learnt the impact of the human activities that are toxic to trees. You have heard birds singing up in them thousands of times. You have walked in many different parks with your friends, along tree-lined paths.

No longer do you perceive a tree as just as a mere mobile thing on earth. It's associated with your memories of things that have been experienced with it. Being an integral part of your life, stored in long-term memory, you have become inseparable from your relationship with the word tree. You have become *proficient* in your memory of trees.

Nevertheless, if someone learning their first language asks us for what a tree is, you would simply translate it word for word, which can only provide a literal meaning, when a concept that could have been so much deeper than the superficial lexical meaning.

Some of us might wish to take it further on the subject of the word tree, willing to take the necessary effort and time to grow their knowledge and skills far greater than average in one particular area. It is within this environment that our depth of understanding ideas and their applications to reality become far more sophisticated and diversified. This can only occur when we regularly and deliberately practice.

After years of our dedication in mastering one speciality comes to fruition, we become capable of constructing and deconstructing profoundly complex ideas and matters in this second language, manoeuvring and reinventing them with great proficiency.

Your specialty may have more to do with physical objects or may be focused on abstractions. Whatever you specialise in, and no matter how complex the nature of your occupation is, the language is there to communicate the idea. Not all ideas and things in life can be translated into language, which is one of the reasons that we can speak the same language, while still finding ourselves puzzled at things that require more than just literal comprehension. The depths of understanding an idea vary from individual to individual. For instance, there must be an enormous gap between my understanding of relativity and Einstein's.

PART 2

Reorientation

Rules

A high level of language proficiency is only achieved by following these principles:

1. Use feelings or emotions to recall information.
2. Prioritise experiential knowledge.
3. Personalise the learning process.
4. Engage all the senses.
5. Love both variety and consistency at the same time.
6. Be aware of how information is conveyed in different forms (including textual, auditory, visual, phonetic, and olfactory forms), as well as the effects each form of communication has on the mind.
7. Build muscle endurance for different input sources (including newspapers, magazines, podcasts, lectures, talk shows, and soap operas) while understanding the difference in discourse.

8. Absorb the cultural aspects of the language, and assure yourself that it's your choice whether to integrate into the culture or not.
9. Let the language be part of your everyday life.
10. Develop a cultural and social identity within the language.

The true factors that affect the second language acquisition process and the rate of progression.

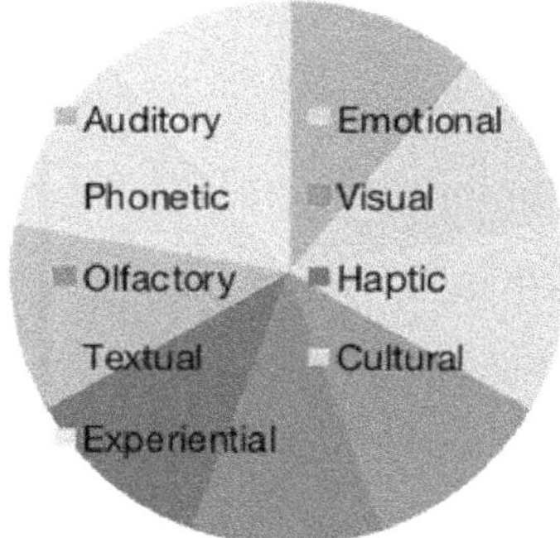

Chapter 14

Text First and Then Visual

Case

You come across an unknown word while reading a text in your second language.

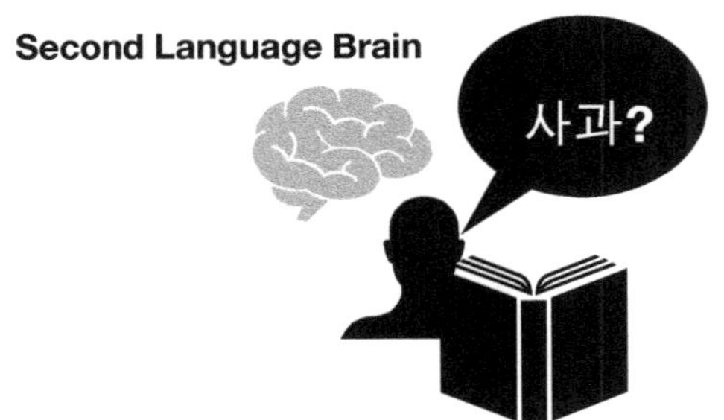

The Existing Knowledge in Your Brain

You would know what the word means in your first language if you were given its physical representation (visual) because your brain already has the knowledge of what the word (in this case, an apple) looks like.

First Language Brain

Your Goal

Your goal is to understand the meaning of the word in your second language without your first language interfering while reading. At the moment, you just have access to the text form of the object (사과) in your second language. If a photo of an apple were provided, the part of your brain dedicated to your first language would immediately retrieve the information from your existing knowledge, before converting the knowledge into text form ("apple").

At present, however, you only have access to the second language text form of the thing (사과), and neither your first nor second language brain is able to tell you what it means. To associate the word with a visual, you need to make the deliberate effort to search for a photo or two, since you cannot consult with your first language brain.

Because you did not the existing knowledge from your first language brain, your second language brain will retrieve information directly from a visual memory chamber separate from your first language brain. This is only possible when your second language brain deliberately fights to occupy a bit of space in your brain where a new image of photographic memory is stored for the direct intercommunication between a word and image in your second language brain.

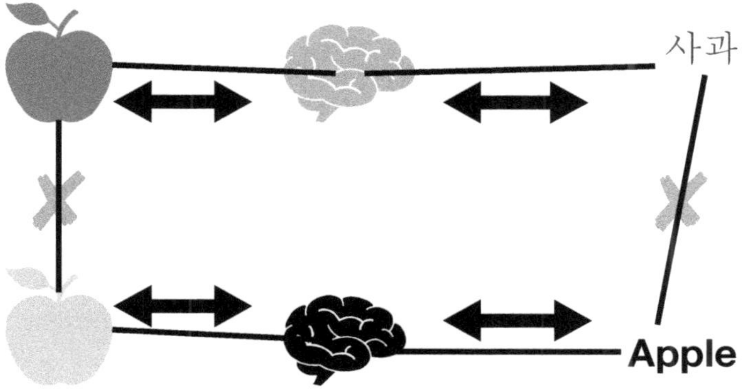

You might ask, *Why not just translate it if we already know what it is in our first language?*

First of all, the brain will not remember things if they are easy to obtain. You need to go through or 'feel' a level of strain as you try to make a mental connection. The brain has a strong inclination for particular kinds of sensations—intense, personal, novel, unique, sensual—while the rest are boring. It reacts to external stimuli most strongly when it experiences these sensations, which trigger the brain's switch for generating the electrical energy to store the information. The more intense and novel the experience, the more electric currents will flow through making neural connections. If the level of intensity is not strong enough, it won't reach the chamber where long-term memory is formed.

Observe and Train Your Mind

Route A
(Slow progress at first, but most effective)

Step 1. Find images relevant to the lexis: Go online and type the language item (words, phrases, expressions, etc.) into Google or another search engine to get relevant images.

Step 2. Try to *mentally link* the image with the language. This takes about 10-30 seconds.

Go directly from text to visual

Go directly from visual to text

Second Language Brain

Step 3. Repeat

Route B

(Fast progress at first, but slow in the long run)

Step 1. Translate text from your second language to text from your first.

Direct Literal Translation without imagining the visuals

Step 2. Check if you already know what the word means in your first language.

I know what an apple is and what it looks and tastes like.

If you already know the concept, all you have to do is to practice the pronunciation until you can convey the info intelligibly. If you have not learnt the concept—meaning you haven't heard or seen of its existence, even in your first language—you should perform Step 2 of Route A, obtaining the relevant visual information illustrating its physical features and shapes.

Step 3. If you do not know what it means or represents, try to *mentally link* the text with the visual in your head. Do it deliberately until your brain is led to believe its existence. In this way of recalling information, your brain will take the following path:

This process is often discussed in neuroscience, although I›d learnt it through experience before I started reading up on such subject. What I mean to say is that, when you focus your eyes (retina), your mind will activated to fire up neurons in the brain, creating a mental connection between the textual and its visual representation in reality. The more you train your brain this way, the faster and easier it becomes over time. Your second language brain will eventually accommodate this way of processing external stimuli until it automatically retrieves the information, even at the slightest trigger. It will drive straight from second language text to the relevant visuals stored in a chamber separate from your first language. Within a nanosecond, it will flash back all sorts of visual memories associated with the textual information.

Unless you deliberately cut a new pathway or neural circuit through which the information is sent to your second language brain, the information will go only through your first language brain. This is mainly because you've only tried textual conversion that only requires textual encoding. You might argue that, if the visual representation of the language item is something that you're already familiar with, why bother? Because what we are trying to do here is force your brain to make a new pathway in which we intentionally make a mental connection between our second language and the fresh visual information, despite the fact that the image represents something that you already know.

What's more important than knowing what it represents is your deliberate attempt to make that connection, creating a new neural pathway that provides access to things that are only associated with your second language.

Caution

Resist the urge to perform purely textual conversion, translating from word to word (Route B). Most people choose Route B for its obvious convenience without realising much of what it does to their brains. It may make thinking and feeling a lot easier at first because it's already been habituated to the first language's neural circuit (route), which is where all of information processing has occurred up to this point in your life. In the long run, however, you won't be able to fully acquire a language; you will certainly be able to process your second language quickly enough, which will make you think you are fluent. Without an established neural pathway that is exclusively for processing your second language, all you can improve is speeding up the rate of translation from first to second or vice versa. This is a dead end, since you will always have to rely on your first language to process the second. If you want your brain to have direct access to visual information so that it can progress straight from text to visual without involving your first language brain, you must first claim a new territory where your second language brain can engage itself in the process of interlinking the textual and visual information, establishing new pathways.

Results

With repeated encounters and exercises, your brain will recall the image at sight of the text or the other way around.

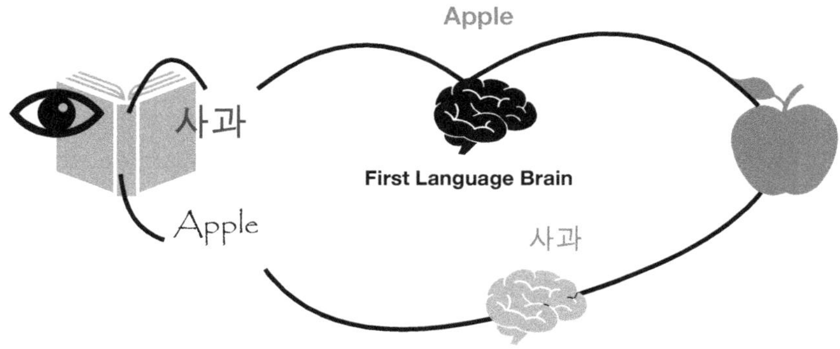
Apple
사과
First Language Brain
Apple
사과
Second Language Brain

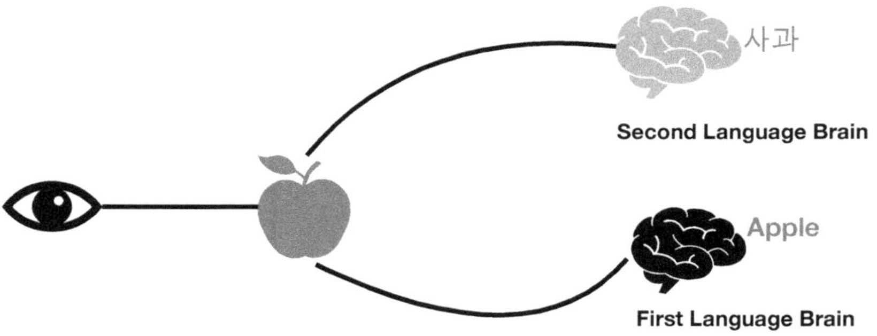
사과
Second Language Brain
Apple
First Language Brain

Chapter 15

Visual <-> Sound <-> Text

Situation

You are walking down the street with your friend. You spot apples for sale as you pass by a fruit stand. You'd like to buy one, but you don't know what apples are called in your friend's language, Korean.

Your Goal

Your goals are to perceive the physical object in your second language without any interference by your first language, and to process its visual information only through your second language.

Imagining and Absorbing

Step 1. *(Option A)* Translate the visual into your second language and learn its name as well as the phonetic and textual components of the object.

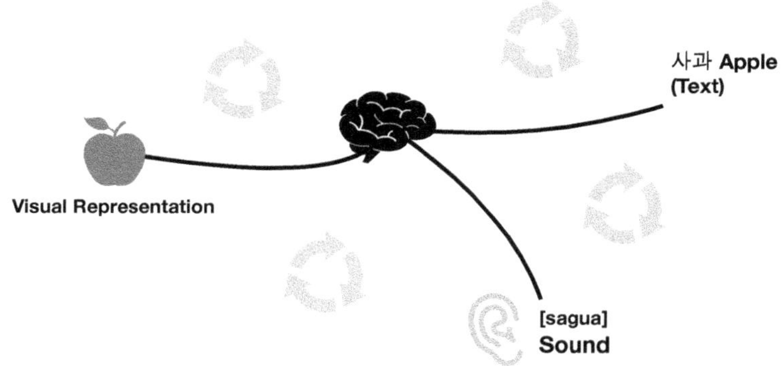

(Option B) Use body language, such as pointing your finger, then wait for your friend to say the word for you.

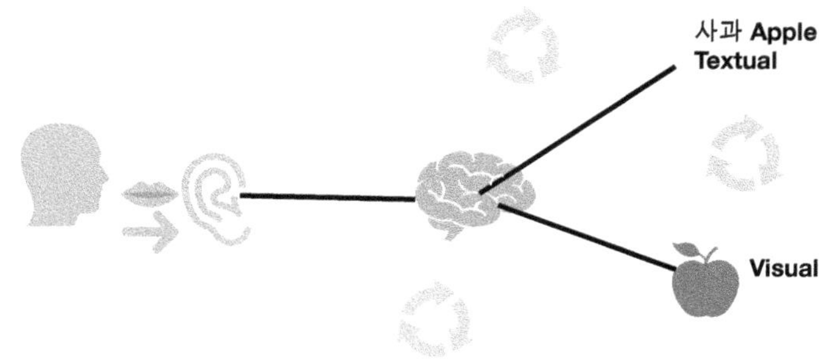

Step 2. Deliberately and repeatedly expose yourself to the same object.

Step 3. Read the word aloud to support your phonetic memory, while trying to mentally connect the thing's phonetic components with the visual. Play it out in your head regularly, using your imagination, or experience it as frequently as is required for you to remember it effortlessly.

Results (up to this point)

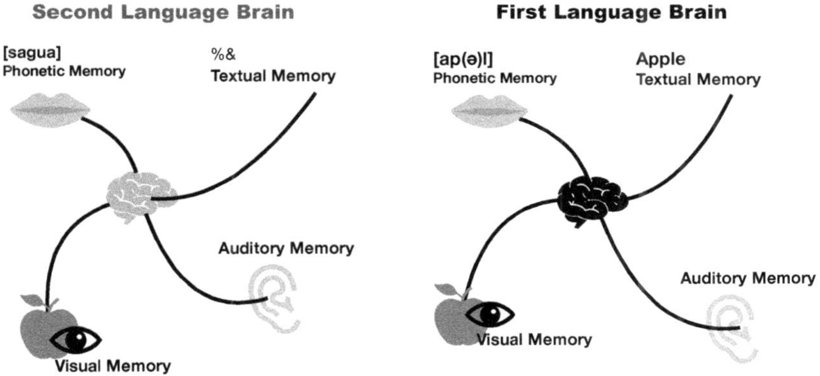

Phonetic	You are able to produce and utter the components of the word
Textual	You are able to recognise the word and meaning
Visual	You are able to recognise the appearance
Auditory	You are able to recognise it when hearing it.

With daily practice, your brain will recall the associated textual, phonetic, auditory, and visual information the instant you experience the relevant stimulus.

Keep in mind that the order in which you're exposed to and obtain the new language varies depending on individual circumstances. You may first *hear* it (reception: auditory) from a YouTube video or podcast episode, and then you want to make your own video (production: phonetic). You might come across a new word while reading a book or script (reception: textual) and then try to write your own (production: textual). Or it may be your professor's lecture where you carefully listen to every single word and then you're assigned to make your own lecture on the subject (production: phonetic). Whichever comes first or whatever order you'd have to follow, your ultimate goal is to make that mental connection across all areas of receiving and producing language. Only then can the information flow interchangeably across all of your senses—phonetic, textual, visual, and auditory.

Chapter 16

Cultural Fluency

Reality

Imagine a situation where you do not understand the concept of a physical thing or abstract idea because it does not exist in the culture of your first language. For instance, let's assume that an apple is perceived only as a fruit, an edible commodity in your country; there are no other possible interpretations nor are there any ways of conceptualising them. You've never heard of Apple Inc. or its products like the iPhone. The scope of your understanding of the word 'Apple' is limited to the concept of it being an edible commodity.

Goal: Reconceptualisation

Your goal is to expand your existing knowledge of the concept so that you will be able to understand how it is perceived differently in the community of either your first or second language. If you succeed, your level of understanding of the concept will be equal to that of a native speaker. At the same time, you will have developed the ability to explain the conceptual difference in your first language to your compatriots.

Observe and Train Your Mind

Step 1. Try to understand how native speakers of your second language perceive it through experience. For instance, listen to them talking or read books they have written on the subject.

Step 2. Stay positive and accommodating so that your brain will not resist. Accept the new concept as it is perceived in your second language's culture and let your brain store the information into your second language's vocabulary repertoire.

Step 3. Deliberately and regularly put yourself in situations where you can experience the same or similar thing (immersion). Be ready to get your hands dirty while having fun.

Step 4. Produce the language on your own. We can see this in the case of Soju and Kimchi:

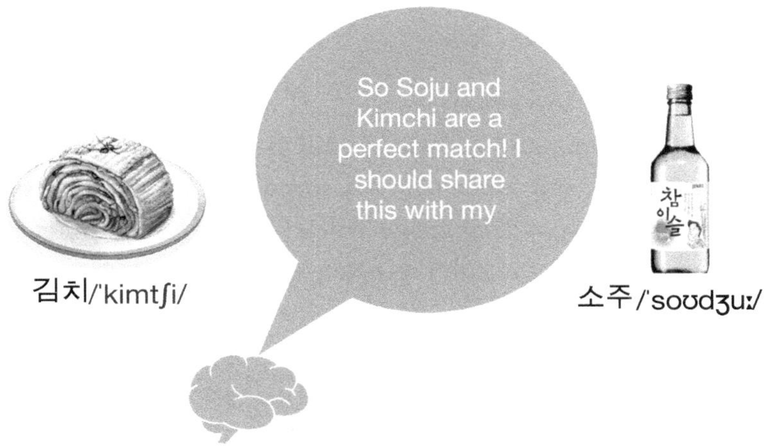

Results

One (short term)

When you see the item, your subconscious mind will receive not only its visual orientation, but also all of its cultural implications and perceptions.

Two (long term: 5-10 years)

Having lived immersed in your second language for a while, your second language brain's capacity has exceeded that of your first language brain. In other words, you know more things in your second language than your first.

Three (long term: 10-15 years)

Although you understand the thing in your second language, you are unable or struggle to communicate the idea to your compatriots exactly the way it is.

Four (long term: 15+ years)

Your experience and knowledge will increase in amount, richness, complexity, and sophistication, surpassing that of your first language. Your second language will eventually supplant your first if you don't use the latter as often as the former.

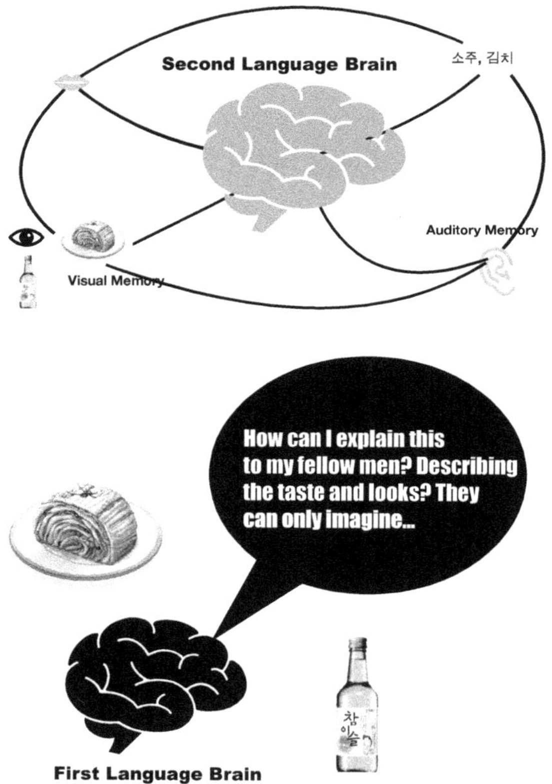

Chapter 17

Second Identity

If you have overcome all of the obstacles in your way and have learnt all of the things described in this book, you should be able to create another identity in the other language. The identity will be activated and set in place once you're in the culture associated with it. Your subconscious mind will act like a silent sensor that can instantly trigger a switch based on your immediate environment—this transition will occur without you realising it.

Whether to make your new identity primary or secondary is up to you. You can stick to your first identity or you can move away for a while and live with your second.

Remember, you may feel these identities as who you truly are. That may be true for the time being, but you have a choice. You can either stay put and complacent or move on to create another one.

Chapter 18

Experiential Memory: Expertise

Reality

By this point, I am assuming that you've reached a standard level of fluency. You are capable of communicating about most physical things and even abstract ideas to the point that you can function at an acceptable level in society. In other words, your ability to verbalise physical and abstract representations has been successfully developed to a level that satisfies the common criteria for the general communication of information. Your literacy is unexceptional, just as your abilities to perceive, reflect, and express are limited-to-average. That's it. No further progress has been made from there. The way you think, speak, and write is just like any others living in the vicinity.

For instance, imagine that someone asks you, *Do you how many galaxies are out there in the universe?* What would you say? You would begin a search in your head and maybe a random number will come to mind, or you may simply say, "I don't know."

Does this mean you are less fluent than those with the correct answer? Just because you are unable to answer a question that requires specialised knowledge? This is where one must differentiate fluency and knowledge.

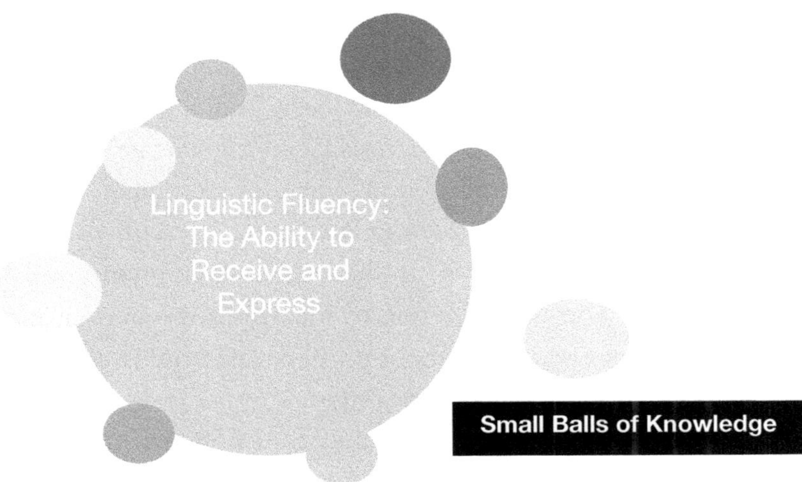

The Ability to Receive and Express

Language production involves both motor movement and timing, and, once acquired, it stays in your brain. The neutrons necessary for receiving and categorising external stimuli have been linked to the eyes for visual perception, the ears for receiving auditory information, and the nose for sensing smells. You also have neurons in your brain that are closely connected to your vocal cords, as well as your hand and finger movements, allowing you to both speak and write. These neutrons are localised in your brain, meaning that a particular region of the brain is responsible for a specific function—for instance, the ability to speak. If the part of the brain that is responsible for oral production is damaged, you will lose the ability to speak. But that's enough neuro-scientific talk for now.

Simply speaking, you have stored all the rules of the language regarding its grammar and vocabulary. You have a huge database of information stored in your brain that you use as reference points for making appropriate word choices and finding suitable circumstantial and social behaviours, bodily gestures, facial expressions, and common courtesies. Such knowledge is permanent, unless you've suffered a brain injury. It's permanent because you've successfully interlinked the language both with your limbic system and neural circuits to the brain, which involves all of your senses. If you miss any one of the senses in your learning process, the memory of information will be less firmly established in your brain and, thus, easier to forget.

So that's what it means to be fluent. Although you may not know the number of existing galaxies in the universe, it doesn't mean you are any less fluent in the language than the rest of your compatriots. Your ability to express objects and ideas is still in effect; you just didn't have the knowledge to answer such a question. You could make up a number, though.

I think it's 100,000 galaxies.

That's a perfect sentence: subject, verb, object. Whether the answer is correct or not by current research does not matter. What this tells us is that your knowledge, what you know, remains at the level of a layman, including what every average person knows. You have a standard level of linguistic fluency, but you're not competitive, as you've nothing much to offer other than your ability to use the language at a standard level.

Goal

Your goals are to be able to gain an expert level of understanding, to employ the terminologies of an area of specialisation, and to communicate them to the masses.

Experiential and Non-Experiential

Let's go back to the topic of outer space. Can you experience an extraterrestrial environment? Can you rent a spaceship and leave the Earth? Your answer is mostly likely *No*, unless you're one of the select few astronauts chosen for such a profound mission. Not everyone will have the opportunity to physically experience what average people perceive to be abstract concepts, such as space. In this way, most of us are observers or spectators in many areas of life.

Advice

Since my expertise is limited to the subject of second language acquisition, all I can tell you regarding the selection of a specialisation is the following. If you've developed a second identity through another language and now you're looking for ways to further develop yourself beyond the average level, you must *choose* a specific area of expertise. That's obvious. What is most important is that your approach to developing an expertise must be based on the idea of becoming a new self and integrating it into your life. You must not let experience or circumstances determine who you will be. You must choose and transform beyond who you are now in the same way as you acquired your second language. From then, immerse yourself in the area of your expertise for a lifetime. Again, up to this point, what you have accomplished is not just about having learnt another language. You've mastered such a variety of ways of employing all of your senses mentally and physically. You know what is the key to learning something effectively.

Final Results

You have developed an expertise and your linguistic repertoire is specialised in a particular field. Your experience within the domain is substantially above average. The general public will listen to your words, as you're providing an invaluable service to the masses.

At this point, the focus should no longer be on improving verbal fluency, but rather on prioritising the gaining of more experience specific to career or business development—the kind that will help you stand out in your area.

About the Author

Jun Namgoong is a writer and teacher who currently lives in Shanghai. Any questions about the author or his works? Contact him at jng@*diglasia*.com

Diglasia

www.ingramcontent.com/pod-product-compliance
Ingram Content Group UK Ltd.
Pitfield, Milton Keynes, MK11 3LW, UK
UKHW021934200726
13853UKWH00011B/1976